FOREWORD

As the governance of universities and higher education (HE) colleges in the UK evolves, there are major implications for members of governing bodies: increasing expectations about how they undertake their role; a greater focus on measuring institutional performance with associated implications for information and strategy; coming to terms with an increasingly complex environment in which governance takes place; and so on. All this means that governors (particularly new ones) need to be well prepared for their roles and the challenges they face, so that they can contribute effectively to their boards from the outset.

...mmissioned by the ...ee of University Chairs[1] ...ced with financial ... in 2009 five volumes ...These were well ...esearch and ...ernationalisation[2].

...e the core information ...ies in relation to ...n, although references

...g governors[3], self- ...'governors' dilemmas'. ...y 'agreed' view of the ...ncourage self- ...lers will agree with ...ted.

...rces for individual ...nt activities; or as web-based material (see www.lfhe.ac.uk/governance). The text does not consider the broader issues concerning the overall responsibilities of governors and how their effectiveness might be determined. Readers interested in this should consult an earlier companion volume called 'Getting to Grips with Being a Governor'[4].

A note on terminology and diversity

As most governors know, governance in UK HE is complicated by the use of different terms for similar functions, so for simplicity some key terms have been standardised throughout all the volumes in the series. The terms 'governing body' and 'board' are used generically to include: the governing bodies of post-1992 HEIs; the councils of pre-1992 universities; and courts in Scotland. Similarly the word 'governor' is used to indicate a member of these

---

[1] See www.lfhe.ac.uk and www.bcu.ac.uk/cuc.
[2] All these publications are available from www.lfhe.ac.uk/governance
[3] The quotations have been obtained from a wide range of sources, including personal meetings with governors. Where the professional background of the source governor is known it has been provided.
[4] Guild HE, (2006), Getting to Grips With Being a Governor, at www.lfhe.ac.uk/governance/govpublications

different bodies, 'chair' is the term for the person who convenes governing body meetings, 'head of institution' is used for the vice-chancellor or principal, and 'executive' for members of the senior management team or equivalent. The phrase 'international students' is taken to describe all those coming to the UK from outside the EU and who pay full cost fees. Finally, the abbreviation 'HEI' is used as the widely accepted shorthand for 'higher education institution'.

It is also important to recognise that the UK HE system is very diverse, which means that some aspects of what is effective governance in one HEI may not necessarily be so in another. Moreover, different governors will have legitimately different views on many of the issues presented in this material, as will heads of institutions and other senior managers. It follows that if after working through the text important issues are raised for governors about practice in their own HEI (and we hope they will be), then they may need to obtain more detailed information from the clerk or secretary of their board or its chair.

Because HE is now the responsibility of the devolved administrations within the UK, another aspect of diversity is the need to recognise differences in governance arrangements in HEIs in England, Scotland, Wales and Northern Ireland. Where no separate discussion of the different jurisdictions occurs, readers can assume that the content applies to all four higher education systems.

How this volume is organised

To provide an overview for governors new to the topic, Chapter 2 explores what internationalisation means for higher education, followed (in Chapter 3) by the strategic implications for HEIs. Chapters 4 to 7 then summarise the many international developments taking place under four main headings: recruitment, partnerships, offshore campuses, and internationalisation 'at home'. The final chapter then pulls the previous content together and provides an overview of the responsibilities of governing bodies in this area - so if governors only want to read one chapter then that is the one to choose!

Disclaimer

The inevitable disclaimer! Although every care has been taken to try and ensure the accuracy of the content of this material, if in doubt about a specific issue governors should always check with the clerk or secretary of their own board.

Happy reading!

Allan Schofield
Series Editor
Spring 2011

CONTENTS

TEN KEY INTERNATIONALISATION ISSUES FOR GOVERNORS

1   Internationalisation is not just about recruiting more international students to try and solve the financial problems of UK HEIs.

SEE CHAPTER 2 ▶

2   Internationalisation affects every part of an HEI and some aspects of it bring potential financial and reputational risk. Governors must be fully informed.

SEE CHAPTERS 2 & 8 ▶

3   Governors should be involved in discussing, approving and reviewing the internationalisation strategy and in assessing its achievement through the use of agreed KPIs.

SEE CHAPTERS 3 & 8 ▶

4   The governing body's responsibility for financial sustainability means it needs to understand the international student marketing strategy and test assumptions about future recruitment and growth.

SEE CHAPTER 4 ▶

5   The governing body must ensure that a satisfactory international student experience and value for money are provided. This should include receiving data and survey results on international student satisfaction.

SEE CHAPTER 4 ▶

6   International partnerships are undertaken for a variety of reasons, and the governing body must understand the rationales, benefits, risks and financial consequences of major strategic alliances.

SEE CHAPTER 5 ▶

7   Because of the reputational risks of poor quality international provision, the governing body will need to ensure that robust quality assurance processes are in place, and the results reviewed by appropriate bodies.

SEE CHAPTER 5 ▶

8   Offshore activities must be closely monitored by the governing body at all stages from concept to performance review, because of the large number of legal, financial and reputational risks involved in both countries.

SEE CHAPTER 6 ▶

9   If an HEI has a policy of promoting the internationalisation of the campus community, a governing body may need to monitor performance in increasing UK staff and student mobility as well as the internationalisation of the curriculum.

SEE CHAPTER 7 ▶

10   The governing body should ask management how they know what international activities are being undertaken, and in what ways the more important ones are monitored and reviewed.

SEE CHAPTER 8 ▶

1. OVERVIEW

1.1 As a governor, how much do you know about the international activities of the HEI of which you are a board member? How much do you think you should know? To start with try answering three simple questions:

- Approximately how many international students has your HEI enrolled this year?
- If your HEI has any international partnerships with universities and colleges in other countries, can you name three of them?
- Have you read the internationalisation strategy of your HEI, and has the board of governors discussed it and approved it? Is it kept under review?

1.2 Now, bearing in mind that the board of governors has "unambiguous responsibility"[5] for issues such as financial sustainability and risk, try answering three more difficult questions:

- Do you and other governors know the full costs and benefits of international activities?
- Has the governing body assessed the current and potential impact on institutional reputational risk of international activities?
- How do international activities fit in with the long term strategy of your HEI?

SUGGESTED TASK

As a governor, how would you answer the questions in paragraphs 1.1 and 1.2? If you don't know, do you think you should?

1.3 Whilst most governors will (we hope) be able to answer the questions in 1.1, those in 1.2 are much more difficult. However, as international activities become ever more important to UK HEIs they are the kinds of questions that governing bodies will increasingly have to think about - if they are not already. This material is designed to help you and others involved in governing UK HEIs to think about the answers to such questions, and also to identify some of the other crucial questions that governors need to ask.

1.4 Of course, not all HEIs and their governing bodies deal with international issues in the same way, so in reading the text and thinking about the questions posed, you need to be aware of some of these key differences. They include:

- In some HEIs governing bodies are actively involved in developing and monitoring the achievement of the international strategy, in others much less so. This may depend on the general engagement of the board on strategic issues, their knowledge of the topic and whether it has previously been seen as an issue for the board.
- Clearly the extent of international activity varies widely between HEIs, although almost all are involved in some way. This has obvious implications for how important internationalisation should be for a governing body.
- The overall mission of an HEI is also likely to influence the extent to which it is involved in international activity: to take an obvious example, HEIs with a primarily local or regional mission may be less involved than others.

1.5 So, parts of this Guide are likely to be of more relevance to some governors than others, but some of it will be relevant to all. Put simply: HE is becoming increasingly

---

5 See the CUC's 2009 Code of Governance at www.hefce.ac.uk/pubs/Hefce/2009/09_14/ The Guide sets out the definitive responsibilities of governors, and is not duplicated in this material but is cross-referred to where necessary.

global, and governors need to be aware of the implications. Another issue could well be that as a governor you think your HEI should be more involved internationally than it is. If you see competitor institutions being very active internationally, you may want to know why yours is not. Your questions might therefore focus on what is not happening internationally in your HEI as well as what is.

1.6   Operating internationally raises new kinds of challenges that may be a worry for many in an HEI. It is not just the financial, cultural and operational issues of international working that may be difficult, but there can also be more headline-grabbing moments, for example, Libya is an obvious example! If an institution chooses to operate in many countries overseas, the chances of staff or students being involved in political, religious or social incidents could be quite high. Have you and your colleagues on the board got an effective risk management process that will take account of all aspects of international operations?

2. WHAT DOES INTERNATIONALISATION MEAN?

2.1   In the past many people in UK HE have appeared to think that internationalisation was about getting more international students to plug the gap left by poor national funding. This material aims to show that this should not be the case, and perhaps the key message from the following pages is that internationalisation is not just about recruiting as many international students as possible; indeed the damage done to UK HE by such a view is summarised later.

2.2   In fact, with the rise of globalisation the word 'internationalisation' is coming to mean all the activities that have international implications. HEIs now tend to produce 'internationalisation strategies' rather than international strategies, since the latter term tended to focus only on the recruitment of international students. In this chapter internationalisation is defined, along with a summary of why many countries see it as increasingly important and promote it.

The wider definition of internationalisation

2.3   If it is accepted that internationalisation means more than recruiting international students, there needs to be agreement on what it includes. Increasingly HEIs are adopting the definition used by Jane Knight (a specialist in the area)[6] that "internationalisation is the process of integrating an international/inter-cultural and/or global dimension into the goals, functions, teaching, learning, research and services and delivery of higher education".

2.4   Putting this idea into practice means that a fully internationalised HEI is likely to have most of the following features:
- A significant proportion of international students.
- Offshore teaching activities delivered in some form.
- International collaboration in research.
- Academic staff from many nationalities.
- An internationalised curriculum.
- Social and academic integration between UK and EU/international students.
- Staff and student mobility and study abroad activities.

In the following chapters each of these areas is explored from the perspective of how much governors need to know, and what potential financial and reputational risks exist.

2.5   Two more definitions may be useful, and make a distinction between 'internationalisation abroad' and 'internationalisation at home'.
- *'Internationalisation abroad*' is about the flow of staff and students both to and from the UK, strategic alliances with international partners, joint programmes with overseas institutions, overseas campuses, and so on.

"Time was, the term international education really meant study abroad and applied to a relatively few students or professors… Times have changed… Few indeed are the institutions that do not offer an array of international experiences to students."

RICHARD SKINNER
TRUSTEESHIP, MARCH/APRIL
2009 pp 9
www.agb.org

---

6   Knight J, (1994), Internationalisation: Elements and Checkpoints. Canadian Bureau for International Education, Ottawa

- '*Internationalisation at home*' concerns issues such as: internationalising the curriculum, recruiting international academic staff, adopting the Bologna principles (see below), and enhancing the quality of the international student experience in the UK.

Attention is often focused on internationalisation abroad as it is the more financially lucrative of the two areas, but most UK and EU students will not study overseas and so benefit most from internationalisation at home. This is the less studied area, but the one which potentially will bring the greatest benefit to students.

2.6 Finally, whilst dealing with definitions, let's get one more out of the way: 'trans-national education (TNE)' is an increasingly used term which means the delivery of education in another country (eg through partnerships), and a very large number of UK HEIs do it.

The motives for internationalisation

2.7 So at the outset there is a key question: why internationalise and why are governments encouraging it? Some of the answers can be found in the following quotations from the national policy documents of the UK's major competitor countries:

Australia: "The benefits of international education go far beyond the immediate economic contributions made by students who come to Australian universities to undertake their studies. International education enriches and changes Australian education and deepens relationships between nations. These social and cultural benefits are clearly of paramount importance in a world where international relations are undergoing rapid changes, and where Australia's future depends critically on its ability to establish diverse and productive international connections"[7].
USA: "In the long run those who can move seamlessly between different nations, cultures and languages will be positioned to capitalise on the next scientific, technological or information revolution"[8].
Canada: "Canadian universities readily acknowledge that providing students with international knowledge and intercultural skills is now an integral part of their institutional agenda"[9].

2.8 Many more such quotations could have been produced, but in short, almost all countries see internationalisation in HE as a key way of ensuring that graduates emerge with an understanding of other cultures and a willingness to work internationally. The International Association of Universities (IAU)[10] gives a very broad rationale for internationalisation in the quotation in the side box.

2.9 The IAU surveys the reasons why countries believe in internationalisation, and in the last survey in 2009 the reasons given in order were: increasing economic competitiveness, developing strategic alliances (political, cultural, trade, academic etc),

"To fulfil its role effectively and maintain excellence, higher education must become far more internationalized; it must integrate an international and intercultural dimension into its teaching, research, and service functions. Preparing future leaders and citizens for a highly interdependent world, requires a higher education system where internationalization promotes cultural diversity and fosters intercultural understanding, respect, and tolerance among peoples. Such internationalization of higher education contributes to building more than economically competitive and politically powerful regional blocks; it represents a commitment to international solidarity, human security and helps to build a climate of global peace."

INTERNATIONAL ASSOCIATION OF UNIVERSITIES (SEE FOOTNOTE 10)

---

7 Universities Australia (2009). Press Release in October commenting on commissioned report on the benefits of international education at www.universitiesaustralia.edu.au/page/ media-centre/2009-media-releases/benefits-of-international-education
8 American Council on Education (2002) Beyond September 11th; a comprehensive national policy on international education at http://store.acenet.edu/showItem.aspx?product=309401&session=66F0CE5B61664BAE9A58D3AF31A0CFD5
9 AUCC (2008). Internationalization: a force for change at Canadian universities at www.aucc.ca/policy/research/international/survey_2007_e.html
10 IAU (2000).Statement on Internationalization: towards a century of co-operation. Adopted by the 11th IAU General Conference at www.iau-aiu.net/p_statements/ i_statement.html

building human resource capacity, promoting international cooperation, furthering cultural awareness and understanding, and strengthening educational export industries. It is worth noting that a financial justification is ranked last.

2.10 To date the UK government has generally supported internationalisation in HE, the most visible evidence being the two Prime Minister's Initiatives. The first (PMI1) in 2000 was a five year programme that aimed to increase the UK's market share of international students. The second (PMI2) began in 2006 for another five years and had broader aims to:

- Better position the UK in the global student market, increasing HE recruitment by 70,000 and further education by 30,000.
- Double the number of countries sending more than 10,000 students to the UK.
- Show improvements in the satisfaction ratings of international students with their UK experience.
- Achieve significant growth in the number of strategic collaborations between UK and overseas universities.

2.11 Alongside these actions other initiatives of the UK government and/or stakeholder bodies have included:

- Opening offices of the research councils in China, India and the USA with a brief to foster research collaboration.
- Project based funding for HEIs to promote academic links with India, China and the USA.
- Further funding under the INSPIRE project[11] to explore strategic partnerships with countries such as Afghanistan, Bangladesh, Kazakhstan, Pakistan and Uzbekistan.
- Other programmes (some managed for government by the British Council) include a link programme with Russia (BRIDGE)[12], support by the English government for England-Africa programmes, and a Whitehall government fund for general development of academic links (DeLPHE)[13].
- Until 2009 there were relaxations in visa and work permit regulations in England so that foreign students could work in the UK for up to two years after completing their study. This brought England into line with Scotland and the USA. However this policy has now changed (see Chapter 4).

2.12 Within the UK various bodies support the efforts of HEIs in this area. The main ones that governors may come across are:

- The British Council, which amongst other things provides an advisory service for HEIs through its network of over 100 overseas representative offices, and acts as a recruiting and marketing agent for many HEIs (for a fee). The Council owns and develops EducationUK as a marketing brand for all its education services overseas. (See www.britishcouncil.org)
- The UK HE International Unit which produces regular intelligence on the international market place for international students and international partnership opportunities, and maintains a restricted website with briefing notes on target countries. (See www.international.ac.uk)

---

11 INSPIRE is a British Council funded project that aims to strengthen academic and research partnerships between UK HEIs and those in Afghanistan, Bangladesh, Kazakhstan, Pakistan and Uzbekistan.

12 The UK-Russia BRIDGE partnership programme (between 2004-08) aimed to establish and strengthen academic links between the UK and Russia.

13 Development Partnerships in Higher Education (DELPHE) is a Department for Internal Development (DFID) programme aimed at using partnerships to help to fight global poverty.

- The UK Council for International Student Affairs (UKCISA) which acts as a watchdog for the interests of international students in the UK. It also provides advice and training for university staff involved in student recruitment. (See www.ukcisa.org.uk)
- In Wales, the Wales International Consortium (WIC) acts on behalf of all Welsh HEIs in coordinating overseas missions to recruit students and develop international links. (See www.walesinternationalconsortium.com) In Scotland the same role is undertaken by the British Council.

2.13   The UK Border Agency is a recent player on the scene, and some might argue with the suggestion that it 'supports' UK HEIs in the recruitment of international students. Its role is to administer the visa system for international students, but some aspects of current visa policy are controversial, and - at the time of writing - felt likely to reduce the numbers of international students in the UK (see Chapter 4).

A summary of some key international developments

2.14   Of course, many other countries have taken similar initiatives, and there is almost a competitive race to internationalise by attracting world class researchers. For example, Canada has a very generous scheme of attracting global applicants to research chairs with promises of up to C$10 million for each chair over a seven year period. Australia has a similar scheme to attract younger researchers, also with generous funding.

2.15   The national drive to internationalise HE is not confined to the West. For example, in China and Malaysia the ministries of education are actively promoting the recruitment of international students and the development of strategic international partnerships for their HEIs. Similarly, Singapore has seen itself as a regional hub for many years, and has adopted a policy of encouraging leading world class institutions to establish campuses in the city state, with Yale University being expected to develop a liberal arts college with the National University of Singapore[14]. Elsewhere, Saudi Arabia has amazed western researchers with the vast $10 billion endowment made available to the King Abdullah University of Science and Technology (KAUST) to establish a world class research capacity. A very long list of such examples could be provided, but the point for governors is clear: to look outwards beyond the UK.

A few words on Bologna

2.16   The phrase 'Bologna Process' may be familiar to some governors, but probably should be known to rather more[15]. That it has not been given the same attention in the UK that it has received in other countries is probably due to the fact that it has required relatively little change on the part of the UK to conform to its principles[16]. In short, the Bologna Process sought to establish common approaches to the delivery of aspects of HE amongst its signatory countries.

2.17   A 'stocktaking' of what the Bologna Process entails and the progress made by each country was undertaken in 2009[17], and shows what each has achieved in ten strands

"If the university were a curry, then internationalisation would not be an additional ingredient - it would be a spice. It gets everywhere and changes the flavour of everything, often in unpredictable ways."

PROFESSOR AT JAWAHARLAL NEHRU UNIVERSITY, INDIA

---

14   University World News. Issue 148 21st November 2010.
15   The UK Europe Unit has produced a useful guide to the Bologna Process which is at http://www.europeunit.ac.uk/bologna_process/index.cfm
16   For an outline of these and what the Process aims to achieve see http://ec.europa.eu/education/higher-education/doc1290_en.htm
17   See www.ond.vlaanderen.be/hogeronderwijs/bologna/conference/documents/Stocktaking_report_2009_FINAL.pdf page 122

of the three broad areas of the Process: the introduction of a two cycle degree system and a national qualifications framework; national external quality assurance reviews; and taking steps towards recognition of achievement with diploma supplements and links to a European Credit Transfer System. The 'stocktake' showed that Scotland had implemented all ten aspects of the framework, but England and Wales still have further work to do in HEIs adopting the diploma supplement[18] and introducing more international participation in national quality assurance mechanisms.

2.18   The most recent development has been the launching in March 2010 of the European Higher Education Area involving 46 Bologna signatory countries including many outside Europe[19]. It aims to achieve "comparable, compatible and coherent systems of higher education throughout Europe".

Conclusions

2.19   Since internationalisation cuts across almost every institutional activity and is being practised by most competitor countries, it is important that governors understand what it is, why it is happening, and what their HEI is doing about it. Therefore the rest of this Guide takes governors through all relevant aspects of internationalisation, to see where the benefits, the potential pitfalls and the risks are lurking.

Self-challenge questions

*   By way of an introductory question: what do you think are the main challenges facing your HEI in relation to internationalisation activities?
*   What are your own HEI's main objectives for engaging in international activity?
*   Having read this chapter, do you consider that your HEI's objectives are in line with those set out by government and some international organisations, as summarised above?

---

18   For a simple explanation of what a Diploma Supplement is see the Guide produced by the UK Europe Unit at www.europeunit.ac.uk/sites/europe_unit2/resources/GuideDS.pdf
19   For more information about the EHEA see www.ehea.info

3. INTERNATIONALISATION STRATEGIES

3.1   In this chapter the reasons why HEIs want to internationalise are summarised and some examples of their internationalisation strategies given. Your role as a governor in reviewing the strategy is summarised in Chapter 8.

Why are HEIs internationalising?

3.2   There have been several recent surveys of the internationalisation strategies produced by HEIs, and some describe their rationales for internationalising. The following is a selection of quotations about their motives[20]:

- "To develop an international ambience on all campuses through targeted increases in the number of international students".
- "To contribute to the development of graduates who are employable globally", and "enable people to understand the links between their own lives and those of people throughout the world" and "work towards a more just and sustainable world where power and resources are more equitably shared".
- "For the university to be celebrated as a premier internationalist university for professional policy, practice and applied research".
- "To develop students' international opportunities and global perspectives, ensuring that an international multi-cultural ethos pervades the university".
- "To embed and sustain an active international culture that fosters cultural awareness, provides opportunity for international collaboration for staff and students and develops understanding of global issues".
- "Create a strong brand for the university as a distinctive international university with a strong European focus amongst all staff, students and stakeholders".
- "To strengthen [X] as an international university through partnerships.... that will strengthen the recruitment position and income base of the university".

These motives tie in well with the findings from the 2009 IAU survey of national motives cited in Chapter 2.

3.3   What is interesting about these statements is that only one institution mentions income generation as a motive. This is probably because there has been a shift in thinking towards regarding internationalisation as much more than recruiting international students. Of course, no-one denies that having international students on campus may be beneficial financially, but few HEIs now say so openly in their strategies.

3.4   Most internationalisation strategies have adopted the definition given in Chapter 1 by Jane Knight, however, there can be a key difference in their focus, with an emphasis either on increasing the international reputation of the institution or concentrating on developing students as global citizens.

3.5   In practice, this means that some strategies are primarily *institution centred* while others are *student centred*. The former applies to institutions that seek to promote

"I think there are real dangers in over-estimating the short term financial benefits of internationalisation of higher education. But if you look more broadly, there is clear evidence and a recognition of the benefits that international students bring to teaching and learning."

PROFESSOR CHRISTINE ENNEW, PVC FOR INTERNATIONALISATION, UNIVERSITY OF NOTTINGHAM CITED IN THE TIMES HIGHER EDUCATION, 8 NOVEMBER 2010

---

[20] Taken from: Council for Industry and Higher Education, 2008, Global Horizons and UK Universities at www.cihe-uk.com

themselves globally, and they usually see the need for a select number of high level international research partnerships to strengthen their institutional reputation (and possibly their position in the global and domestic league tables). By comparison student-centred institutions tend to explore issues such as the internationalisation of the curriculum or the need for students to study abroad or learn a foreign language. What they are likely to have in common is the wish to recruit more international students and have a higher proportion of international academic staff. HEIs with student-centred strategies are more likely to emphasise teaching and - in general - be in the post-1992 part of the sector.

3.6 Of course, the two types of strategy are not mutually exclusive, and as an example, one HEI has combined both strands in the following compact strategic statement: "our vision is to be celebrated as London's premier internationalist university for professional policy, practice and applied research, dedicated to preparing students for global careers, and working with global practitioners, research and educational partners".

Integration with other strategies

3.7 There are many strategy documents in HEIs, usually written at different times by different people and in response to pressing internal or external factors. As a result a governing body should be on the lookout for inconsistencies between them and seek explanations, although, in practice, it may be very dependent on its secretariat to find them.

3.8 The most significant document is, of course, the overall corporate or strategic plan, and subsidiary strategies should fit with it. This link is particularly important for the internationalisation strategy, as it is usually all embracing and will have a close relationship with many aspects of an HEI's other strategic priorities. The box below suggests some typical links between an internationalisation strategy and others:

STRATEGIC AREA	LINK TO THE INTERNATIONALISATION STRATEGY
Overall corporate plan	Umbrella strategy for all other strategies. How does internationalisation support the mission and key targets?
Teaching and learning strategy	This might include: internationalisation of the curriculum; provision for foundation and English language training; any offshore teaching activity in partnerships or franchises (including relevant quality assurance); international student support; the adoption of a policy of study abroad for students; etc.
Human resources strategy	This might include: policies on recruiting international staff; the pay and conditions of UK staff working overseas; equal opportunity and diversity practices; the weight given to international work in promotion criteria; etc.
Financial strategy	Included in this will be: the costs of investing in offshore activities and partnerships; international student recruitment costs; on-campus investment in improving the experience of international students; etc. International students' tuition fees will be a key element of the HEI's income.

"How are international experiences administered on campus? Are they essentially cottage industries, the product of individual faculty members' initiatives and effectively 'islands' of activity with little coordination or institutional management?"

RICHARD SKINNER
TRUSTEESHIP, MARCH/APRIL
2009 pp 13
www.agb.org

STRATEGIC AREA	LINK TO THE INTERNATIONALISATION STRATEGY (CONT...)
Research strategy	This might include: the development of international collaboration and research partnerships; international knowledge transfer; etc.
Estates strategy	This might include: the suitability of the environment for international students; accommodation for international staff and students; etc.
Communications and marketing	Boosting the HEI's international reputation will be a core aim of this strategy as it will assist both the recruitment of students and the formation of quality partnerships.
Alumni and development	This normally includes ways of informing international alumni about HEI activities, and using them as ambassadors or even sources of employment for returning graduates.

What does a good internationalisation strategy look like?

3.9   Most internationalisation strategies are relatively recent and typically have two common features: the assumption that increasing the recruitment of international students is possible, and a statement about the importance of international partnerships. Otherwise strategies differ greatly in the extent to which they include activities on campus ('internationalisation at home').

"In general, the Council's lay members would like to see a more strategic approach to overseas ventures, with a clear rationale based on our academic and financial interests and values."

GOVERNING BODY CHAIR

3.10   At a minimum an international strategy might contain most of the following information:

- The objectives of its internationalisation activities, and the link to institutional mission.
- A recognition of current strengths and weaknesses in relation to internationalisation.
- Priorities for future action over a defined time frame with a stated rationale.
- The general criteria for selecting partners and 'doing business'.
- Commitments to ethical recruiting and behaviour.
- An overall risk analysis, including the definition of risk appetite.
- The identification of key performance indicators (KPIs) and other general targets.
- An outline of the financial requirements for strategy implementation, including a commitment to full economic costing.
- A general outline of implementation challenges and an indication of action required to address them.
- Proposals for review and evaluation, including the definition of any exit strategies that may be necessary.

3.11   As an example, Annex C provides the internationalisation strategy of the University of Surrey, chosen (with permission) because it is comprehensive and sets clear milestones and targets where appropriate.

3.12   Not only should the governing body formally approve the international strategy, but - in general - it is also desirable for it to discuss a draft strategy, and some HEIs do this at a strategic awayday. Without such engagement, it can be too easy for board approval to be sought too late in the day to influence major new proposals, or for it to be seen as acting as a 'rubber stamp'.

3.13   The other aspect of strategy is, of course, monitoring and measuring its achievement, and as a governor you will want to know how well the HEI is doing with its international strategy. As noted above, it is desirable for strategies to include agreed performance indicators - a few of which may be particularly important as KPIs.

3.14   Some of the indicators that could be applicable to your HEI's internationalisation strategy (and are used by other institutions) are:
- Number and quality of new strategic partnerships agreed annually.
- Number and quality of fully operational strategic partnerships.
- International students as a percentage of the total student population (with separate figures for UGs and PGs).
- Improvement among international students in their satisfaction scores with the HEI.
- Numbers of international students offshore studying for the HEI's degree programmes.
- Numbers of home students studying or working overseas.
- Percentage of academic staff born or educated outside the UK.
- Percentage of students who have learned a foreign language while with the HEI.
- Numbers of students who have participated in optional programmes covering topics related to global citizenship.
- Proportion of the curriculum that has been reviewed against internationalisation criteria.
- Research funding generated from international sources.
- Change in ranking in the international league tables.
- Increase in number of incoming international academic visitors.
- Number of research papers and articles/citations co-authored with international partners.
- Volume change in the international media coverage of the HEI.
- Number of staff presentations at international conferences.

3.15   Typically the management of an HEI will have proposed KPIs from the above list (or something similar) to suit the particular aspects of a strategy, but it is important that the governing body discusses their suitability and ensures that they are rigorous measures. More detailed operational indictors will also be used by management, but these will typically be too detailed to be of concern to governors. Of course, as with all indicators some things are more easily measured than others, for example assessing an HEI's aim to develop its students as global citizens will be particularly difficult.

3.16   As an illustration, one university has set a goal for its international profile as one of the four strands of its corporate strategy and has agreed some performance targets for achieving it.

Corporate goal:
"To raise our international profile by developing strategic partnerships, increasing the visibility of our research and teaching, strengthening our alumni networks and influencing policy on global issues."

Performance Targets
"Our performance targets for the international profile are:
• Top 100 in world university rankings.
• 30% of our student population from non-UK countries.
• 30% of our faculty from non-UK countries.
• 25 strategic, sustainable international partnerships with universities, organisations and agencies in other countries."

Internationalisation and risk

3.17   The internationalisation strategy can have very significant risks, although these will - of course - depend on the kind of activities involved. On the one hand the development of offshore activities (particularly those involving substantial investment) will feature high on a risk profile and should be of active interest to the governing body, on the other hand if internationalisation consists mainly of modest academic links and teaching partnerships, then the governing body may not be directly involved other than through the oversight of standard risk management processes.

3.18   In general, financial and legal risks should be well recognised by governors - particularly members with commercial or professional experience - who should require the usual financial and investment disciplines to be applied to any overseas venture. More problematic is reputational risk, and various HEIs have found that their reputation in particular countries has been damaged because of problems not identified early enough. Perhaps the crucial issue for governors is to ensure that proactive review mechanisms are in place for all major internationalisation activities, and are reported through appropriate routes. Passive acceptance by a governing body that all is well because no problems have been reported is a recipe for a disaster waiting to happen, as some HEIs have found out to their cost. The separate guide in this series on risk provides more information on how to do this.

3.19   Progress on the implementation of the internationalisation strategy and mitigating associated risks also needs to be monitored by the governing body. In some HEIs this is done by an annual report (which includes the extent to which any agreed key performance indicators have been achieved), thus providing the board with a useful opportunity to discuss key issues as they arise.

Implementing and managing internationalisation strategies

3.20   Although governors will not be involved in the management of internationalisation strategies, they do need to be aware of the basic management processes used, and how monitoring and reporting is undertaken. In most HEIs a member of the senior management team (SMT) is responsible for internationalisation, but this is often not the only name in the job title. Thus the role of pro vice chancellor (PVC) international (or similar) is commonly linked with other responsibilities such as teaching and learning, external affairs, etc. The key requirement is that this person is held accountable for coordinating the development of the internationalisation strategy, for monitoring performance against any targets that have been set, and for reporting them to the governing body.

3.21 It is increasingly common to find two levels of management committees or task groups involved in the implementation of internationalisation. The first tends to be concerned with strategic issues and monitoring, and will usually consist of SMT members and senior professionals (and may be called 'internationalisation strategy committee' or similar). The second is more operational and oversees issues such as staff and student mobility, proposed partnerships, and the coordination of overseas recruiting. Governors are unlikely to hear anything about such operational issues, but might expect to receive occasional reports from the strategy group.

3.22 Typically, the operational aspects of internationalisation will be undertaken by a support structure which has become increasingly professionalised, with an international office responsible for all aspects of marketing and recruiting international students, and some of the support functions for them once admitted.

3.23 Such international offices are gradually increasing in stature and responsibility, and in some HEIs job titles for their heads are emerging such as 'director international' or similar. With these titles has come a widening of responsibilities beyond the core role of marketing and recruitment of international students, which now often include:
  · A partnerships office, covering both UK and international links.
  · The management of study abroad and staff/student exchanges.
  · International student support on campus including the delivery of English language teaching.
  · Managing any overseas representatives, including agents.
  · All matters relating to incoming international visitors, including 'meeting and greeting' and organising visitor programmes.
  · Relationships with international alumni.

3.24 However, there is no standard model for the way that support for internationalisation is organised; nor any recognisable structural differences between large and small HEIs. Almost all HEIs have international offices but what they do varies widely, as does the seniority of the person heading them, and the number of staff[21] (but an international office with between 20 and 40 staff is not unusual).

3.25 There is, of course, a limit to what the central management can achieve in the implementation of internationalisation, and there will be heavy reliance on deans and heads of departments to deliver in areas such as research collaboration, promoting student mobility, student and staff exchanges and internationalisation of the curriculum. Even in the area of recruiting it is likely that there will be some overlaps between the work of the international office and the marketing activities of each faculty. Indeed, in many UK HEIs it is very hard for an international office to monitor and coordinate overseas visits and activities undertaken by faculty and departmental

"Formally our mission is to be a university which is highly active internationally, but I'm not sure that the Council knows what that means, or if we have ever discussed it in detail. It's true that we did approve a paper given to us by the executive, but that was near the end of a long meeting with lots of other business."

EXTERNAL GOVERNOR OF A LARGE HEI

---

[21] A report in 2008 for the UK HE International Unit on 'The practice of internationalisation: managing international activities in UK universities' explored the different models of international offices – see www.international.ac.uk/resources/The%20Practice%20of%20Internationalisation.%20Managing%20International%20Activities%20in%20UK%20Universities.pdf

staff, and a typical management response is to set up various internal networks to try to establish some order and ensure that activities follow the agreed strategy. Thus, an HEI may have country groups of enthusiasts for China or India meeting at intervals, or formal networks of faculty staff charged with overseas recruiting.

3.26   One consequence of the difficulties of coordination is that it is hard for any central office to know what is going on. Collecting data on international contacts is not easy, and there is a risk that overlapping visits will be made to countries or that ill-informed collaborations may be started with unworthy partners. Some HEIs insist that all overseas staff travel is recorded centrally (using the rationale of collective insurance cover) and this enables them to know who travelled and to which country; however this is resisted in other cases. Of course, an SMT does have one mechanism that it can use to encourage a coordinated approach to internationalisation: funding. Many HEIs have created central resources which can be made available to finance international activities, sometimes in the form of funding pots to which faculties make bids.

Self-challenge questions

*   Have you read the internationalisation strategy of your HEI?
*   Is the strategy primarily institution-centred or student-centred (or both) and is this appropriate?
*   Is the international strategy wholly compatible with the overall strategic plan?
*   Do you think that the internationalisation strategy has been adequately considered and reviewed by the governing body?
*   How do you monitor the internationalisation strategy and assess whether it is succeeding?
*   Does the governing body fully understand the risks involved in implementing the internationalisation strategy?

A GOVERNOR'S DILEMMA 1:

The papers for a forthcoming meeting of the governing body contain a proposed internationalisation strategy, that has been approved by the senate/academic board. However, the governing body has a long agenda, and it is clear from the papers that a major discussion is not planned; indeed it appears that the management expects it to be 'rubber stamped' by the board. You have some major concerns since you think that the institution is not active enough internationally and should have a higher proportion of international students - for both cultural and financial reasons (at present 6% of your students are from outside the EU). You also feel that the internationalisation strategy does not make enough of the potential of international academic partnerships to widen the horizons of both staff and students. What should you do?

4. THE RECRUITMENT OF INTERNATIONAL STUDENTS

4.1 Just how dependent is your HEI on international student income? Is a fall in numbers a key risk? Is there a danger of more recruitment being at the expense of student quality? As a governor how can you be sure that your HEI is recruiting students ethically? These are some of the issues considered in this chapter.

Some statistics

4.2 Globally the number of students travelling to other countries is over 3 million pa. Of these 21% go to the USA, 13% to the UK, and 9% to France. Many UK HEIs are dependent on such students for their financial survival. The numbers are large: in 2009-10 there were 280,760 international students (11% of the total) in UK HEIs, compared to 22% for Australia and 3.5% for the USA. Postgraduate recruitment is strong, and in 2009-10 accounted for 27% of all such students. There are also about another 50,000 international students studying HE programmes in private colleges, but no statistics are available[22]. In addition, 125,000 students come from the EU.

4.3 Care is needed when interpreting international data as different definitions may be used. EU students are the problem, and are counted along with domestic students in all UK publications (as they are treated like UK citizens and do not pay international fees). However, international statistics often conflate EU and non EU students, to make the data comparable with that of other nations.

4.4 Taken together, international and EU students are heavily concentrated in a few disciplines, as the Table 1 shows[23]:

TABLE 1: NON-UK (IE INTERNATIONAL AND EU) STUDENTS IN HE BY SUBJECT OF STUDY 2008-09

	NUMBER OF NON-UK STUDENTS	% IN SUBJECT WHO ARE NON-UK
Business & administrative studies	101,715	31%
Engineering & technology	46,055	31%
Social studies	31,365	15%
Computer science	22,190	23%
Languages	21,265	16%
Subjects allied to medicine	20,480	7%

4.5 Some HEIs have become large scale recruiters of international students, and Table 2 shows the top ten recruiters in the UK in 2008-09.

---

[22] See the recent report on private sector provision in UK HE by CHEMS Consulting for Universities UK. At
www.universitiesuk.ac.uk/Publications/Pages/Privateandforprofitproviders.aspx
[23] Source = HESA, Statistical First Release 153. January 2011

TABLE 2: INTERNATIONAL STUDENT RECRUITMENT BY HEI 2008-09

INSTITUTION	NON-UK STUDENT NUMBERS BY HEI (FTE)	% NON-UK STUDENTS BY HEI (FTE)
The University of Manchester	8,800	23%
The University of Nottingham	7,900	24%
University College London	7,125	34%
The University of Warwick	7,080	25%
London School of Economics and Political Science	6,555	68%
The University of Oxford	6,020	25%
London Metropolitan University	5,810	22%
University of the Arts, London	5,750	20%
The University of Leeds	5,690	18%
The University of Northumbria	5,650	17%

4.6   According to 2008-09 data, the leading non-EU countries from which the UK recruits its students are: China (47,000), India (34,000), Nigeria and the USA (14,000 each), Malaysia (12,000), Pakistan and Hong Kong – SAR (9,000 each) and Canada, Taiwan and South Africa (5,000 each). The general trend is for a greater growth in the numbers from India which may soon overtake China as the primary source country.

4.7   Although the absolute numbers coming to the UK have increased, the UK's share of the global total has fallen slightly since 2000[24]. (The USA share has also fallen from 25% to 19.7%.) This is due to the growing competition from countries such as France and Germany, and within Asia from China and Malaysia. China is a dramatic example: it sends 144,000 of its students overseas, but now 195,000 students from other countries go to China[25].

4.8   The significance of these figures is that governors and HEIs should not assume that the numbers of international students will always increase, and internationalisation strategies that target ever growing numbers coming to the UK could prove to be wrong. There are several potential hazards:
   - Students could be deterred by an aggravating system for obtaining visas. This is a global issue but other countries are very aware of the deterrent effect of strict immigration controls.
   - An economic collapse in the major sending countries could radically affect the numbers wishing to study in the UK.
   - Some countries resent the UK's overtly commercial attitude to marketing HE, and their governments may tend to favour other countries where the fees are lower.
   - Increasingly European countries such as France and Germany are teaching courses in English.

[24] According to the OECD it is now 11.6% as opposed to 11.7% in 2000.
[25] These figures relate to 2008 and can be found on the website of the Institute of International Education at www.atlas.iienetwork.org

- Some other countries have greater flexibility in allowing international graduates to continue to work after they have completed their studies. Students like to think that they can get employment in the host country after they graduate.
- Student satisfaction could decline with significant reputational consequences.
- There is growing competition from private providers targeting international students at tuition fee levels that undercut HEIs.
- A scandal involving international students could trigger a national exodus, for example the attacks on Indian students in Australia in 2008 has had a substantial effect on the numbers.
- The UK's reputation for a quality higher education could be damaged by any significant cuts in expenditure or by rash recruitment action by one prominent HEI.

4.9 The implication of these trends is that governors should be cautious about financial forecasts predicting increasing income from international students. The UK HE sector has enjoyed a favourable market position so far, but one of the most likely scenarios is that although international student numbers will increase, it will not be at the rate seen in the past.

4.10 Another issue to think about is whether any limits should be placed on the numbers of international students.[26] Many come to the UK not only to gain a qualification but also to improve their English and learn about us, and if they only meet other international students their experience may be diminished. This may raise important issues for some departments, for example, does it matter if almost all the postgraduates in a department are international? It may be keeping a flagging department alive, but if there is little UK demand for the subject would it be better to close it? To address such issues, some HEIs have set a cap on international numbers in some departments. Whilst primarily operational questions, governors should expect assurance that they are being answered.

How international students are recruited

4.11 HEIs are using increasingly sophisticated methods to market themselves and recruit international students, typically including:
- Direct recruitment via an HEI's website.
- Direct recruitment through an HEI's regional offices overseas. Some institutions have very large networks of such offices and many have a base of some kind in China and India. These offices visit feeder schools and partner colleges, place local advertisements and select students.
- Direct recruitment through face to face meetings at overseas trade fairs or recruiting missions, usually by staff from the international office.
- Recruitment through local agents who market an HEI, find potential students, carry out preliminary vetting of their qualifications and English language capability, and assist applicants through the visa process. In return they receive a commission from the fees paid to the HEI. The British Council's offices in-country also act as an agent for some HEIs.
- Recruitment by companies who then provide foundation programmes (see below) on campus.

"Having traditionally drawn students who are comfortable with the English language, the UK is now competing with non-English speaking countries offering tuition in English."

STUDENT DECISION MAKING SURVEY 2010.
THE BRITISH COUNCIL
www.britishcouncil.org

SUGGESTED TASK

What is the largest proportion of international students that is sensible for your HEI to recruit, and why?

---

[26] Note that the imposition of any quotas on a country basis could be deemed to contravene Part III of the 1976 Race Relations Act.

SUGGESTED TASK

As a governor you will want to be assured that your HEI only engages in ethical recruiting. In practice, how do you know, and how do you obtain the necessary assurance?

4.12 One issue that might increasingly concern HEIs is how ethical are the approaches being taken to recruiting - particularly but not exclusively by overseas agents. Although primarily an operational issue, there are some governance issues here, for example are the practices used by agents known about and actively monitored? As is evident from the quotation in the side box (from a distinguished American commentator on HE) the practice does carry reputational risks. The new Bribery Act has implications for governing bodies in this area[27].

4.13 The choice of recruitment method is usually made by the international office and there are arguments for and against each of the approaches listed above. Clearly, choosing an agent is potentially risky, as a few may be too interested in their commission to apply rigorous filters and quality checks on candidates. There is also a risk that they may oversell an HEI. The recent UK visa processes have proved challenging for some agents, and governors will want to be absolutely sure that lax (or even criminal) behaviour by the occasional rogue agent does not impact negatively on an HEI's reputation. The senior manager responsible for international recruitment should be able to assure governors that all the agents used are reputable and fully informed about the institution. Some HEIs have an annual UK conference of agents so they meet key staff and can be brought up to date with campus developments.

4.14 Growing numbers of students (principally taught postgraduates) are being brought to the UK as part of partnership arrangements with overseas institutions. These tend to be of two main kinds:
   * Students coming for the second or third year of a course where the first year has been delivered in-country to specifications established by the UK HEI. These are called '1+2' arrangements, but a variant is the '2+1' where the first two years are in the country with the final year in the UK.
   * Taught and research postgraduates coming to the UK under research partnership arrangements where the whole undergraduate course is in-country, but the postgraduates work with a UK department which has staff who know and have worked with their partner department.

4.15 A key decision for management is where to focus the marketing effort for international students. Almost all HEIs are putting substantial effort into China and India where there are large numbers of students able and willing to pay, and governors might ask if this is wise. The competition there is huge - from Australia, the USA and even many countries in mainland Europe, so might it not be more cost effective to look at other markets such as Brazil, Indonesia or Vietnam? However entry into these countries will have an upfront investment cost. Such issues will be discussed in setting the international strategy, and governors will want to know that there is a rigour to the marketing effort, that it is based on up-to-date data, and not spread too thinly among a large number of countries.

4.16 Should governors wish to know more about the markets in many of the target countries, the best source is the data and reports published by the UK HE International Unit[28]. However this is held in a secure part of their website accessible to all HEIs and you will need help if you want to access the material.

[27] The 2011 Bribery Act specifically mentions governance issues concerning overseas agents.
[28] See www.international.ac.uk.

Tuition fees for international students

4.17 When HEIs were first allowed to charge tuition fees to international students, the logic was that the fee should enable institutions to recover the full cost. For a period the government set a limit to what could be charged, but that has now gone and there is a general market. Each year Universities UK surveys HEIs to find out what is being charged, and in 2009-10 the range and median undergraduate fees were:

	CLASSROOM-BASED	LABORATORY-BASED
Lower to upper quartile range	£8,500 to £10,000	£9,300
Median	£9,500 to £12,800	£11,500

Each year governors should be asked to approve the next year's fees for international students, and boards will probably wish to see how their HEI compares with others, using the UUK survey.

4.18 An important issue is how competitive UK fees are for international students. The answer is 'not very', and the UK is generally more expensive than Australia and the public sector in the USA. The only institutions that typically charge more are the private universities in the USA and some of the private foundation course providers in the UK. In mainland Europe very few HEIs charge significant fees, and in some countries tuition is free for both international and domestic students. Other factors that students will bear in mind are the cost of living in the UK and the relative strength (or not) of sterling.

4.19 In determining a recruitment strategy, the question of financial support for poor international students arises. A few UK HEIs take the view that it is anomalous to promote access policies at home for those who would otherwise be unable to enter HE, and yet set international fees which only wealthier students or parents can afford. These institutions tend to promote available national scholarship schemes, and are also gradually increasing their own internal scholarship funds to support poorer students from overseas.

4.20 It is always assumed that international students are a source of considerable net income, but this claim can be misleading and should be scrutinised by governors. The government and funding bodies continue to emphasise the importance of full economic costing for teaching and research, and TRAC data now provides some evidence to support this[30]. TRAC identifies the full economic cost of a student in each subject area, and although these will not be entirely coterminous with an HEI's course portfolio they do give a starting point for detailed course costing. For international students there are some readily identifiable 'additional' costs of 'doing business' such as:

- The staffing and running costs of the international office, and any overseas offices.
- Commissions to agents and any fee discounts to students.
- Travel and marketing costs of fairs and exhibitions.
- Advertising in foreign newspapers.

"With all the press coverage of cuts to higher education budgets in the overseas press, there is a real concern at whether the UK will be able to continue to offer the best value for money compared with competitor countries...With these sort of [fee] increases institutions are going to have to invest even more time in improving the student experience to continue to attract good numbers."

DOMINIC SCOTT
CEO OF UKCISA
QUOTED IN THE TIMES HIGHER
EDUCATION, 29 JULY 2010

---

[29] See www.universitiesuk.ac.uk/Newsroom/Facts-and-Figures/International-student-tuition-fees/Survey-results-2009-2010/Pages/Default.aspx

[30] For an explanation of TRAC see www.jcpsg.ac.uk and www.hefce.ac.uk/finance/fundinghe/trac/tdg

- Specific on-campus costs attributable to international students (eg an English language centre).
- Social and welfare services aimed at international students (eg meeting and greeting at airports).
- A proportion of standard overhead costs incurred in supporting all students.

This will mean that the TRAC calculated costs are less than the true full costs which the institution will need to take into account when determining an adjusted full cost. Such an exercise should be carried out on an annual basis.

The UK Border Agency and Highly Trusted Sponsor Status

4.21   A great deal of heat has been generated by the activities of the UK Border Agency (UKBA) which is a spin off from the Home Office charged, among other things, with keeping terrorists out of the UK. In 2009 it devised a new points based system for monitoring incoming students. To enter the UK with what is called a 'Tier 4 visa', students require an HEI or other qualified UK educational institution to sponsor them, and also need to score enough points to be accepted as an international student in the UK. Forty points are required, with 30 awarded for attending a course at a recognised level with an approved institution, and 10 for having funds to cover course fees and costs of living. The system grants visas for an initial period which is dependent on the length of the course. In general, a Tier 4 student can stay in the UK for the length of the course plus four months (for courses lasting a year or more) or one or two months (for courses between six months and a year). For shorter courses, international students are only granted a week to stay in the UK once the course has finished.

4.22   The 2009 system required students to be vetted by the UKBA before coming to the UK - a problem as the exercise was cumbersome. However the process was simplified in 2010 by the UKBA's creation of the status of 'Highly Trusted Sponsor' which has been automatically awarded to all publicly funded HEIs and some of the private providers. One of the conditions of being a sponsor relates directly to the rationale for the whole system: that the UKBA wishes to ensure that all foreign students are genuine and not economic migrants who do not intend to study, or terrorists. Therefore the sponsor must undertake to tell the UKBA if an international student fails to enrol or withdraws from their studies. Highly trusted sponsors must also ensure that students do not miss contact with tutors, and are asked to undertake two extra registration processes a year for international students.

4.23   All this is clearly controversial, but if an HEI were to lose its sponsorship status it would be very serious, and - in practice - it could no longer recruit foreign students. This is a new risk, and governors will need to ensure (perhaps through internal audit) that management has developed systems to monitor student attendance. Some private providers (see below) issue students with biometric passes and expect them to log their presence at every lecture, but it is doubtful if this will be copied by many HEIs.

4.24   Another area where the English government and UKBA could have a major impact on the recruitment of international students is if the policy on their being able to continue in England after their studies and take up paid employment were to be hardened - as is proposed. Policies in this area are a major discriminating factor between countries. For example it is much easier for international students to stay on in the USA, while in Australia there have been restrictions on the numbers able to seek employment, and these are having a significant impact on the numbers of international students applying to Australia. If England follows Australia and makes it more difficult for international students to obtain employment after their studies, it is very likely that the same thing will happen.

4.25   In mid March 2011 the Whitehall government announced an easing of earlier UKBA proposals on restricting student visas and post-study employment, but the whole issue remains fluid. This adds to the general uncertainty about forecasts of future international student numbers and the potential for continued growth.

International students in associate private colleges

4.26   HEIs increasingly have agreements with other providers, validating courses and awarding qualifications taught by others. This increasingly includes the validation of private colleges, which now provide courses in subjects such as business, law and hotel management. There are at least 200 such colleges which offer awards validated by at least 60 publicly funded HEIs, and it is possible that around 50,000 international students are studying in this way, although there is no accurate data.

4.27   A particular issue in this area is that many international students need remedial English tuition before starting their studies. Although HEIs will have set a required minimum admissions standard in one of the two main international tests (eg an IELTS score of 6.5)[31], these are not always foolproof, and some international students will under-perform because of poor language skills. Because of this almost all HEIs provide English language support, often in specialist centres spun off from the languages departments.

4.28   There is a trend for this support to be provided under external contract, and five private companies now offer HEIs such a service. By the end of 2010 over 40 HEIs had implemented such arrangements, which may also include recruiting students, offering study skills and providing a foundation year in relevant disciplines. The normal model is for the private provider to build or rent an associate college on an HEI's campus where the international students will live for a year and be treated as full students. Most HEIs who have entered into such arrangements find that their international student numbers have grown dramatically because of the global marketing capacity of some of the companies concerned.

4.29   This service may be run either as a simple contracting out arrangement or by developing a joint venture in which each party shares some risk, and some of the private providers prefer the second approach. Whichever model is adopted, the key point is that an HEI needs to be clear about its accountability and risk. Thus, the key issues in the contractual negotiations tend to be:
  • The quality of provision and its assurance.
  • That the curriculum is always in line with that for comparable students entering from other sources.

---

[29] The International English Language Testing Service (IELTS) is a major provider of over 1.4 million English tests each year and is widely used by UK HEIs. The other major test is TOEFL (Teaching Of English as a Foreign Language) and is American.

- That the overall student experience is at least as good as that for other students.
- The integration of the company's marketing effort with the HEI.
- The terms and conditions of staff who transfer to the provider.
- A management structure that gives the HEI adequate control of and input into key decisions.
- A financial return that justifies the risks involved.
- The ability to terminate the contract as necessary.

4.30   In general, the experience of HEIs that have used such providers has been very positive, and at a time when international recruitment is vital for financial survival the resources and overseas networks of private companies can be a valuable addition to the international marketing programme.

Keeping international students satisfied

4.31   This chapter started by noting how competitive the international student market is. It is therefore important that HEIs do their best to ensure that international students are treated well and have a satisfactory experience. If this is not the case, critical feedback will rapidly appear on the many facebook or web sites devoted to student opinion. In addition to the generic issues affecting all students, there are many specific things which can go wrong including:
- Students feeling ghettoised if they are all placed in an international hall of residence.
- Failure of tutors to provide the attention expected.
- Disappointment with aspects of the student experience.
- The alcohol culture of some HEIs which may alienate students.
- Possible tensions with the local community, particularly in large HEIs which may dominate their local communities. This may occur even when the presence of international students can be shown to bring significant economic benefits[32].
- An HEI failing to provide value for money for the fees involved.

4.32   Accordingly, it is important to know what your international students think, although they are not a homogeneous group. The National Student Survey (NSS) is not helpful as it does not distinguish domestic from international students. Accordingly, some HEIs collect their own data, and many subscribe to an annual survey of international student satisfaction run by i-graduate, a private company that also collects data in New Zealand, Australia, USA, South Africa, Germany, Singapore and the Netherlands with over 150,000 students involved[33]. If governors are concerned about their HEI's international student reputation they might ask for data on how their performance compares with others, and if an HEI does not use this survey, governors might seek clarification from management about how they judge international student satisfaction. Further information is provided by UKCISA (the UK Council for International Student Affairs)[34].

---

[32] See for example: Oxford Economics: The economic impact of the University of Exeter's international students (April 2010) www.exeter.ac.uk/international

[33] See the details of their International Student Barometer at www.i-graduate.org/services/student_insight--student_barometer.html

[34] See www.ukcisa.org.uk

Self-challenge questions

- How dependent are your HEI's finances on recruiting international students? Is there any form of Plan B if the numbers were to fall?
- Are your HEI's student recruitment targets realistic given the institutional track record so far?
- Has your governing body been provided with a full economic cost analysis of the financial picture concerning international students? If so, what are the implications?
- Do you know how your HEI recruits its students, and do any of the methods used put its reputation for ethical recruitment at risk?

A GOVERNOR'S DILEMMA 2:

As you walk around the campus you see a lot of international students, but they appear to be always in national groups and do not seem to mix much with the domestic students. This worries you as you had thought that the institution was selling itself as a friendly place where incoming students could meet UK students and learn about our culture. You are worried that the apparent failure to achieve this could lead to negative feedback from the present cohorts of students that would deter future applicants from their countries. How should you express these concerns?

5. INTERNATIONAL PARTNERSHIPS

5.1 Almost every internationalisation strategy mentions overseas partnerships, a term which can cover many different types of relationship. This chapter considers aspects of partnerships that concern governors, including: types of partnerships; key implementation challenges; ensuring financial sustainability; and risk.

5.2 The focus of the chapter is mostly on trans-national education (TNE): teaching an institution's programmes offshore. TNE is a growing part of academic life, and approximately two thirds of UK HEIs have some provision[35]. HESA now collects statistics on the number of TNE students, and in 2009-10 reported some 408,685 international (not EU) students studying for over 1,500 UK awards and registered with a UK HEI but located outside the UK; this is much more than the number of international students in the UK.

5.3 Both teaching and research partnerships are becoming more strategic, and HEIs typically choose to be allied with a small number of partners in either teaching or research or both. This is a trend among all the world's major universities, encouraged not only by governments, but also because international corporations are seeking to do business through global partnerships with HEIs. In one sense this means that the search for good partners is becoming a competitive 'game', and in developing countries institutions are becoming more selective when they look for international partners, and no longer take up every link that they are offered.

Types of partnership

5.4 One way of looking at partnerships is to classify them in terms of scale. A widely used classification which fits all kinds of institution and applies to both teaching and research activities distinguishes between level one, level two and level three partnerships, defined as follows:

- Level one partnerships are primarily strategic, and developed at a senior level within an HEI with the aim of the link becoming deeply embedded institution-wide across a range of faculties and activities, including both teaching and research. Governors may well be involved in approving such partnerships because of the resource implications. For example, Monash University in Australia has decided that it will have just four level one partnerships with carefully selected leading institutions in China, UK, India and the USA.

- Level two partnerships are mainly developed and operated at faculty level to fit particular subject requirements. However, they will often involve professional support from the central administration if flows of staff and students are involved.

- Level three partnerships are individual links between academic staff in different institutions. They are usually based on common research interests, but may also relate to teaching exchanges and short term stays, for example as a visiting professor in an overseas institution. It is almost impossible for management to know about all level three links, and this may not be necessary if there are no major financial or contractual implications. One research-intensive HEI has

"I am really worried about some of the partnerships we seem to be developing overseas, with little thought to our reputation or brand. Almost every set of governing body papers brings information about another one, but the SMT seem relaxed about it all."

EXTERNAL GOVERNOR OF AN HEI

---

[35] Drew, S. et al, (2008a), Trans-national education and higher education institutions: Exploring patterns of HE institutional activity. DIUS Research Report 08 07.

estimated having over 2,000 such links, but decided that it was not worth the effort of logging or monitoring them.

5.5   Research partnerships are a well-established feature of academic life and most academics find that regular contacts with peers abroad are crucial to the quality of their research. A separate guide in this series on research considers partnership issues in more detail, but the key questions for governors are likely to concern the relationship between an HEI's research strategy and its internationalisation strategy, the degree to which the partnership is based on reputational advantage, and the extent to which the full economic costs of international research collaborations are fully recovered.

5.6   Teaching partnerships are often more complex, vary widely between HEIs, and include franchises, joint programmes, and programme validation. The number of such collaborative links is growing rapidly, for example the Quality Assurance Agency (QAA) surveyed UK HEIs in 2009 about their links with Malaysia and found 260 links with 107 Malaysian partners[36].

5.7   In practice, teaching partnerships can have several motives, which may depend on how they are funded. Most commonly they are self-funded and are driven by the desire to generate income either from validation or accreditation fees, or from the flows of students to the HEI after an initial year or two on the HEI's franchised courses with the partner institution. However, others may be supported by public funds (such as DfID or the Commonwealth Scholarships Commission) and a purpose of developing local academic staff and supporting teaching in developing or emerging economies. Once this is achieved, the funding may come to an end.

"What governors need to do is to agree the strategic criteria for partnerships and then let us get on with it. Some of them need to realise that you can't keep bringing operational stuff like approving every last partnership back to them for approval."

A PVC INTERNATIONAL

5.8   The key issue in teaching partnerships is the effect on an HEI's reputation. This can be damaged in several ways: by creating relationships with unworthy partners; by too strong an emphasis on the financial aspects of any relationship; by failing to take cultural norms and practices of the partner into account; and by paying too little attention to the quality of provision.

5.9   In the past the QAA has been critical of the practice of some UK HEIs in relation to quality, and key issues include: which institution provides the award received by students; how quality assurance is maintained; the responsibility for teaching and student support across partners; and so on. As an example, the QAA's audit of UK provision in Malaysia in 2009 pointed out the need for greater consistency of good practice in the following areas in order to avoid common weaknesses:
  - Ensure that policies and procedures for managing collaborative provision are clear and comprehensive, and then stick to them.
  - Have a written agreement and keep it up to date.
  - Prioritise access to effective electronic learning resources for students outside the UK.
  - Maintain close working relationships with the partner, but do not rely on one person to do it.

---

[36] QAA (Sept 2010). Audit of Overseas Provision, Malaysia. Overview Report at www.qaa.ac.uk

- Where relevant, be clear about professional accreditation.
- Give the partner's students and staff effective and timely feedback on their performance.
- Provide support for English language development, even where English is already widely spoken.
- Involve the partner's staff and students in programme management and development as the partnership matures.

5.10   Although a governing body will largely rely on the process of academic governance (including the senate/academic board) to address key academic issues and to oversee the quality of offshore delivery, it will also need to be satisfied that senior management has appropriate mechanisms in place to monitor the quality of what partners are delivering, with any substantial risks being reported. This issue is explored in more detail in the separate guide in this series on academic and student issues.

5.11   Overall, the UK is seeking to correct a reputation it has in some countries for only being concerned with HE as an export business, and for acting in an aggressively commercial manner. Several HEIs are taking a positive approach by treating a partnership as one of equals, where both partners seek to gain equal benefit and the overseas partner is not regarded as a junior.

The partnership life cycle

5.12   Most partnerships at levels one and two begin with a formal agreement such as a memorandum of understanding (MOU) between the partners, which is usually an agreement to start talking about collaboration. It has little legal significance, and although welcomed in some countries in others it is of little value. However it does demonstrate a formal commitment by the institution, and most UK HEIs insist that an MOU can only be signed by a member of the SMT after approval by a Partnerships Office or International Office.

5.13   An important preliminary step that some HEIs take before considering an MOU or any new partnership is to set out a clear policy and criteria on what kind of institution they wish to partner. Since institutional reputations are often judged by the status of partners, it is very important not to rush into an arrangement in response to an approach from an institution that has not been carefully vetted in a due diligence exercise.

5.14   If a major partnership is planned, the governing body should generally be involved, and governors will want to know that potential partners are thoroughly respectable both financially and academically. This is particularly important when considering a link with a private sector body - whether it be a property developer (for example, in relation to a possible new overseas campus), a benevolent conglomerate or a private for-profit tertiary provider. In some countries it is only possible to have partnerships with private institutions, and here, of course, the risks may be greater.

5.15   When selecting an academic partner some of the criteria that governors might be seeking reassurance about are: institutional values; institutional size or matching academic profile; financial stability and respectability; an academic community that is experienced and well regarded; full accreditation by its government; and a similar (or better) reputation than the UK HEI in any national league tables.

5.16   What happens next depends on the type of collaboration planned. After an MOU has been signed (and where it results in a tangible outcome) there will be exchanges of people between the partners to translate the MOU into more practical arrangements. In most cases these visits result in a more detailed legal contract or agreement on the shape of the partnership, defining who is responsible for what, and setting out the implications for quality assurance and finance.

5.17   However, governors should not expect that all MOUs will come to fruition. A large research active HEI may typically have signed many MOUs with potential partners (more than 50 is common and in one case more than 300). However, a much smaller number are likely to become operational as many introductions do not lead to an engagement, let alone the altar. Even when a partnership is up and running, it is very likely that it will change its shape and format at intervals, and it is rare for a teaching partnership to last for more than ten years. One British HEI recently completed ten years of exchanges with a Chinese partner and produced a bi-lingual booklet to celebrate the occasion. This almost turned out to be a wake as collaborative activity started to fade away after it!

5.18   The reasons for the changing nature of partnerships are predictable: the needs of partners change. A Chinese or Indian partner may no longer need support from the UK as the quality of its own standards and facilities grows. Programmes will change and what is marketable in one decade may be unpopular in the next. Most importantly, partnerships are often dependent on personal relationships and the key people who have championed a partnership will move on or be promoted. This is why it is vital to have a deep partnership based on multiple research links with a number of people on both sides.

5.19   What this means is that the status of an HEI's partnerships will never be static. The more substantial ones at levels one and two should be reviewed regularly, as they may need to be culled or closed down at intervals, and it is very important that they do not continue beyond their effective life to become an academic or financial liability. Governors should want to know that someone is asking critical questions about this at intervals, and one way of ensuring this is to ask senior management annually for a report on partnerships and how many have been closed down or withdrawn from in each year.

Financial sustainability and partnerships

5.20   Since the financial memorandum of HEIs makes it clear that the public funding from government is for UK purposes alone, governing bodies have to be sure that offshore partnerships pay their way on a full cost basis. How full cost is calculated is not always obvious, and income from partnerships will depend on the type of collaboration and the agreement signed with the partner. Usually income will be either a flat rate fee for validation and staff development services, or a fee per student taken as a percentage of the tuition charged, or a combination of both. The additional costs incurred in TNE can be substantial, and include not only obvious items such as international travel, and extensive management time in negotiating and managing partnerships, but also

The University of Leeds has defined the criteria for its partnerships as follows:

"a) It should be explicitly contributing to the core academic mission of a faculty or the University ie it should align with our core mission of being a research intensive university that puts the relationship between learning and teaching at the heart of its approach to educating students.

b) It should be with an institution that has a strategy and a reputational profile that adds value to us (and by definition does not detract value) – it should enhance the quality of the University's brand reputation.

c) It should have the potential to increase our academic capacity and/or capability and access new funding to support the acceleration of our academic strategy (at faculty or institutional level) in ways that would otherwise not have been possible.

d) It should make a positive contribution to the University's overall international profile and reputation."

SOURCE: www.leeds.ac.uk/ downloads/file/308/internationalis ation_strategy

SUGGESTED TASK

As a governor, think about a major international partnership involving your HEI which has given rise to significant potential risk. How effectively has the governing body been regularly informed about progress?

in finding replacement teaching staff in the UK. If student numbers fall off, profitability could well be uncertain.

5.21   Accordingly, governing bodies may need to take a long hard look at financial sustainability. By way of example, the University of South Australia has recently decided to stop almost all its TNE, as a detailed analysis showed that it generated more income from its international students on its home campus than from those overseas. The offshore activities were also a source of regular concern over teaching quality. The combination of doubtful profitability and worries about the quality of what was being delivered was enough to sway the decision[37].

5.22   Therefore, because of the costs and risks involved, if your HEI decides to start any major partnership activities overseas (at levels one and two), it is important that the costs and benefits are fully evaluated in a business plan and a risk analysis undertaken. Governors should want to know that there are processes in place to see that this happens.

Self-challenge questions

- Has your HEI got a partnership strategy, and have you read it?
- How is your governing body assured that the HEI's reputation is not at significant risk in any of its international partnerships?
- How reputable are your overseas partners? Is there an effective due diligence process that checks their academic and financial soundness?
- Can you be sure that all overseas partnerships and trans-national activity are viable on a full cost basis?
- Are there effective and appropriate processes for monitoring and reporting the progress and effectiveness of offshore activities to the governing body?

6. ESTABLISHING AND GOVERNING AN OFFSHORE CAMPUS

6.1   The last chapter described the issues of international partnerships, but it is even more challenging from a governing body perspective when a UK HEI decides to set up and operate its own campus or presence overseas. To do this it usually establishes a legal presence in a country from which it delivers education and awards its own degrees. Of all international activities this is the one where there are the most risks and where governors will, understandably, need to be most vigilant. Although there are only about 15 UK HEIs that have formally established offshore bases at present, this number is likely to increase for reasons described below.

6.2   There are basically two kinds of offshore presence:
- A collaborative 'British HEI' or consortium activity. For example, there is already a British University in Egypt, a British University in Dubai, and British Universities in Kazakhstan and Vietnam, although they vary in scale. These are cases where the government of the country concerned has approached the UK government and asked for assistance from British HEIs. A variant of this approach is where a UK consortium such as the NCUK (the Northern Consortium of 11 UK HEIs) has established centres overseas (in China, Pakistan and Nigeria) to deliver foundation programmes for member HEIs. The involvement of an overseas government in such an arrangement has good and bad implications: in theory it should remove or smooth bureaucratic hurdles and may provide funding, but the government may introduce its own regulatory barriers and place limits on operations.
- A sole campus set up by an HEI, usually with help from the national or regional government or a private corporation. There are examples of UK HEIs with campuses in China, Dubai, Greece, Malaysia, Mauritius, Oman and Uzbekistan. One Russell Group HEI even describes its 'international faculty' as being based in Greece. Probably the best known examples of offshore campuses are the University of Nottingham's two operations in Malaysia and China. Both are substantial enterprises with over 7,000 students between them from a wide range of countries.

6.3   Creating offshore campuses is a growing trend and the numbers established have grown by 43% in the five years 2004-09, but the UK is behind both the USA and Australia[38]. Overall the number of such campuses is still tiny when compared with the number of HEIs.

6.4   Why are HEIs doing this? There are several reasons:
- Many HEIs believe that in the future the numbers of students willing to travel to the UK and pay high fees will fall. Having students at the HEI's own in-country campus protects market share and also catches those students who cannot afford to travel to the UK.
- In some countries there is a very large demand for HE that the government-funded HEIs cannot meet.

---

[38] A list of all the known offshore campuses was published by the Observatory on Borderless Higher Education in September 2009 – see Becker, R. International Branch Campuses; Markets and Strategies. at www.obhe.ac.uk

- Some governments actively want HEIs from the UK to set up campuses in their country in order to raise academic standards and help to produce an educated workforce.
- Since most offshore initiatives are principally devoted to undergraduate education, HEIs hope that the campus will produce a flow of postgraduates back to the UK.
- Having a campus in-country enables an HEI to give more emphasis to meeting specific country needs, and may also develop collaborative research. This stance has positive political benefits as the HEI can no longer be blamed for 'milking' the country with high fees for its UK provision.

6.5   An HEI will also need to be clear about the standard of the qualifications to be offered and whether they are intended to be equivalent to those delivered on the UK campus. If the answer is yes, then governors might seek reassurance that this commitment can actually be delivered.

Developing project plans and identifying risks

6.6   The practical, legal and regulatory aspects of establishing an offshore campus vary greatly according to the country and the extent of involvement by the government concerned. However, there are some basic features of all offshore projects:

- Before a project begins, there is a need to undertake extensive due diligence checks on the regulatory environment imposed by the government concerned, which could be hostile and impose financial burdens. For example, the current draft legislation about foreign education providers setting up in India suggests that a deposit of approximately £7.3 million has to be made.
- Most countries have established registration, accreditation and quality assurance regulations that apply to foreign providers, and these will have to be met, as will the requirements of any relevant local professional bodies.
- There are rules in many countries which stipulate that a foreign provider must operate through an incorporated company, which may be required to have a certain proportion of host-country nationals as shareholders.
- The national legislation on the taxation of profits and the repatriation of surpluses may be restrictive.
- In some countries the legislation regarding residence and work permits for foreigners is not flexible enough to allow staff from the UK to work for long periods in the country.
- Private providers of HE are not popular in some countries - and even though publicly funded in the UK your HEI will be classed as private once it operates in another country. So there is often a degree of political risk, which means that a hostile government could cancel any authorisation it has given to an HEI. For example, a few years ago three foreign HEIs were ordered to close down their MBA programmes by the government of South Africa, which was well known at the time for being unfriendly to the private sector and international providers.

6.7   In meeting such challenges an HEI will be able to draw on the experience of other institutions in carrying out such checks, and one obvious port of call will be other

HEIs already established in a particular country. The UK HE International Unit has commissioned a useful guide from Eversheds to some of the legal pitfalls, and has also produced briefing reports on some of the key countries where HEIs want to go[39].

6.8 Once the challenges of working in the country concerned have been assessed, there will be specific project risks to consider and governors should expect to see a rigorous investment appraisal of the venture before giving it the go ahead. This appraisal will probably have to consider extra issues that would not be found in any domestic project appraisal, including:
- Sensitivity to exchange rate fluctuations and exchange control regulations.
- The costs of satisfying the quality assurance requirements of the host country.
- The extra staff costs arising from working offshore. (These may require the HR department to develop new policies on pay, benefits and conditions of service, travel home and accommodation for staff and their families.)
- The overall staffing strategy, since it is very likely that an offshore company will have to employ some local staff and possibly some international academic staff.
- The costs of local consultants to undertake marketing studies to confirm student demand at the required fee rates.
- The extra costs in the UK of undertaking all the set-up and project work from the initial investigation right through to monitoring and evaluation.
- The full range of professional advisers in the country concerned (eg lawyers, accountants and people able to guide the HEI through local bureaucracies).

6.9 As a result, the scale of the technical and professional checks required before setting up an offshore campus can be very significant. In one recent case an HEI that decided to establish a medical campus in another country spent over £700,000 on professional costs in both countries. The project feasibility and plan will have to show that such costs can be recovered.

6.10 Governors should be aware that there may be significant academic and quality issues concerning the establishment of a permanent offshore presence. These will primarily concern the senate/academic board and the other processes of academic governance. In one well known case a UK HEI was invited by the government of Singapore to establish a campus; the governing body was in favour, but the senate was not and voted against the initiative on the grounds of the limitations on academic freedom in the country. This reversal of policy caused some damage to the institution's reputation.

6.11 It is inevitable that any decision to establish a campus will become a local political issue in the country concerned. This introduces a degree of risk and uncertainty and means that your HEI will need to have reliable local advisers. It will not be enough for your campus to have approval from a ministry official in the central government; there are bound to be other layers of bureaucracy involved and these may not always be keen to implement central edicts.

"Frankly, we were bounced into agreeing the venture, because the PVC told us he was going to shake hands on the contract in a few days time."
EXTERNAL GOVERNOR

"Amazingly, some universities enter substantial transactions for operations in foreign countries before they address the laws that apply there. Trouble usually follows."
MARTIN MICHAELSON
TRUSTEESHIP JAN/FEB 2009
pp 23
www.agb.org

---

[39] Eversheds, 2009, International Partnerships; A legal guide for UK HEIs at www.international.ac.uk

How should governors be involved?

6.12   If your HEI wishes to set up an overseas presence the governing body must be involved at three major stages:

- Ensuring that proposals are consistent with the international strategy and the financial sustainability associated with it.
- Ensuring that satisfactory due diligence has been undertaken for the country, any academic or financial partner and the project proposal.
- Reviewing and stress-testing the final project proposal.

In all these stages management should have prepared adequate documentation to support the case; this is not a situation where a summary one sheet of paper will do. By way of detailed review, the governing body chair might ask a small task group to devote time to reviewing the proposal on behalf of the full board. Whilst avoiding detailed management, a project of this kind is an instance where it is worth detailed board scrutiny and challenge, particularly if any member of the board is familiar with the country concerned.

6.13   Among the issues that a governing body will wish to question (and that management should be able to answer) are:

- What are the objectives of the venture? Is this proposal the best way they can be achieved?
- What is the exit strategy and are there opportunities to get out of the project, if political or financial problems occur?
- Is the HEI adequately insured against all the risks that can occur offshore - particularly those affecting students?
- Have all the risks been covered in a thorough risk assessment, with rigorous due diligence and preparatory studies?
- Has the HEI thought through all the implications of its duty of care to the students on the overseas campus?
- What threats are there to the HEI's reputation from the project?
- Is management sure that the quality of the education that is delivered offshore will be as good as that in the UK?
- Are all relevant legal issues covered such as: which law will apply to the contract? Can the contract with the government or partners be written under appropriate UK law? Will intellectual property from research carried out in the country be protected?

6.14   In practice, many HEIs have found that it is harder to generate profits from overseas ventures and then repatriate them than they thought. Indeed, some with experience of offshore activities no longer claim financial returns as their main objective, talking instead of the reputational advantage of contributing to the economic and social development of the host country. Partly as a result, in most recent cases the governing body has decreed that there should be no UK capital contribution to overseas project investment, with the HEI relying on a foreign government or commercial partners to build infrastructure and equip facilities. While this provides some comfort to governors, it introduces a new complication into the relationship with partners, emphasising again the need for careful due diligence on their financial standing and reliability.

Once projects are operational

6.15 Once an offshore campus is established, its academic governance can usually be fitted into an HEI's existing supervisory structure with academic audits or quality reviews occurring at intervals. Similarly, financial reporting and monitoring performance indicators should be slotted into regular reporting frameworks. In addition, depending on the scale of a project, a governing body may need to be given a report on progress against the plan each time that it meets (this was the case in two recent major offshore projects by two Russell Group institutions). However the scale of the enterprise could require more than this, and for large projects a comprehensive annual report might be produced for the governing body. Clearly governors must be sure that any losses from an offshore activity are not buried in, or subsidised by, a larger cost centre.

6.16 This chapter began by implying that setting up offshore activities is high risk. This is because there have been some notable failures by HEIs in Australia, the UK and the USA, making it even more crucial for a governing body to be alert when assessing proposals. An experienced project manager of one large offshore venture summed up his experience in the list of 15 'musts' shown below[40]. Some of these send useful warnings to governors on what to look out for:

Lessons learned from running overseas ventures: the 15 musts

- Due diligence is necessary at all times.
- Understand risks at every stage and respond.
- Do not over-delegate, but define responsibilities. Clear lines of responsibility and accountability are required at all times.
- Communicate well and visit the partner country often.
- Recognise that political support does not remove the need to follow and work through the usual systems and procedures.
- An early engagement with the professional and regulatory bodies in both countries is essential.
- One must expect and respect cultural differences and anticipate misunderstandings, as each national context will be different.
- Patience is essential. Allow enough time (and then double it!).
- Make realistic forecasts of the income and expenditure.
- Review and revise plans, budgets and timetables regularly as part of good project management.
- Maintain transparency in all activities.
- Ensure that appropriate legal agreements are in place between all stakeholders.
- Keep complete control of quality assurance and remember the project aims and purpose.
- The venture must be owned and embedded within the HEI at all levels.
- Leadership is vital, but do not rely wholly on one individual. Succession planning and backfill must be built in to the planning from the start.

---

[40] Source: Professor RK Jordan, CEO Newcastle University Medicine Malaysia (with acknowledgement to Carolyn Campbell, QAA). Published in Managing International Partnerships, Research Report, November 2010 by CHEMS Consulting for the Leadership Foundation in Higher Education

Self-challenge questions

- Have governors been adequately involved in the decision to establish an offshore presence?
- Have all stages of the project set-up been fully reviewed by governors?
- Has the project been thoroughly checked to ensure that all the major risks are identified and reviewed as part of the risk management process?
- Has the academic board or senate effective ways of ensuring that the quality of higher education being delivered offshore is maintained?
- If your HEI has offshore activities, do you know whether the original objectives are being achieved?
- If your HEI has offshore activities, does the governing body receive a regular financial analysis, and is the activity meeting financial targets?

A GOVERNOR'S DILEMMA 3:

You have just seen in the governing body papers a reference to an agreement that is being negotiated with the government of Vietnam concerning a possible campus in Hanoi. It appears that proceedings are quite well advanced including an arrangement with a local property and construction company that will develop the infrastructure.

This worries you greatly since through other sources you have had some experience in dealings with the Vietnamese government. There are several areas in which you could contribute to negotiations, and you have also heard unsatisfactory reports about the probity and ethics of the property company.

However, it may be too late for you to help. What should you do?

7. INTERNATIONALISATION 'AT HOME'

7.1 This chapter concerns a less dramatic side of internationalisation: provision at home, including the experience of international students. If your HEI has a student-centred internationalisation strategy, some of the issues below should feature in that. Of course, much of internationalisation at home is connected to the way the curriculum is provided, so it is primarily an issue of academic governance and a matter for the senate or academic board. However, there are areas where governing bodies will have a bona fide interest, such as the quality of the overall student experience, and the recruitment of international staff.

7.2 In Chapter 2 internationalisation at home was defined as including: internationalising the curriculum, the recruitment of international academic staff, the adoption of the Bologna principles, and the quality of the international student experience. This brings us back to the motives that countries and HEIs have for internationalising. Some HEIs have built such motives into their strategic goals, for example, one has produced a booklet on global citizenship[41] which emphasises the benefits for employability cited in the side box.

7.3 Such developments are clearly part of a governing body's responsibility for determining educational character and mission, and therefore raise the strategic question of what the agreed success criteria will be, and how a board can know whether management has succeeded.

Creating an international community

7.4 An important part of internationalisation at home lies in creating a vibrant international community for learning and research. The benefits of this will be immediately evident to most governors, but achieving it in practice may not be easy, particularly in non-campus HEIs.

7.5 Beyond what happens in the classroom or research laboratory, what can an HEI do to create such a community, and how should governors be involved? If the aim is to get the national and international students to mix socially, then an HEI cannot simply place the international students all in the same hostels or residences and hope that they interact with UK students. Nor can an HEI simply rely on its students union, although it should be an important partner in developing such a community.

7.6 Typical actions by HEIs active in this area include providing social spaces that do not rely on alcohol, sponsoring cultural events on campus around particular countries' cultures, and encouraging students to run festivals and events on international topics. For example, in several HEIs students organise large 'one world' events, devoted to describing other societies and cultures, and sometimes fund them through commercial sponsorship. Governors may wish to show their support by participating in such occasions.

"Employers are strongly supportive of our 'education for global citizenship' agenda. We believe we produce graduates who have the skills that will be necessary for professional success in the 21st century - including receptiveness to other cultures and contexts that will equip students to work effectively outside the UK."

UNIVERSITY COLLEGE LONDON, SEE FOOTNOTE 41

SUGGESTED TASK

As a governor, have you ever been asked to attend an international student function? If not why might that be?

---

41 University College London, (2009), Education for Global Citizenship at UCL. www.ucl.ac.uk/global_citizenship

7.7   There are, of course, potentially negative aspects to having an international mix of students and cultures on campus. Some of these relate to the risk that some student groups might be fostering radical thinking, and this calls into question an HEI's powers to question or tamper with the principle of free speech. A governing body has clear responsibilities in relation to the conduct of aspects of student affairs, and should seek reassurance from the executive about any activities of student groups that could be breaking the law. Another risk is that the presence of a large international community on campus could cause ill feeling (or even racist abuse) in some towns and cities. As noted above, this has happened in Australia recently, and it is vital that an HEI has mechanisms and a policy for close and proactive community liaison.

Recruiting international staff

7.8   Internationalisation at home is obviously assisted by the recruitment of international staff, and numbers have grown rapidly in the past few years: in 2008-09 26% of full time academic staff were from other countries. The percentage of young researchers is even higher. Much of this has happened without any deliberate institutional policy due to the free flow of labour in the EU, and the very talented staff from countries in the former Soviet Union.

7.9   Whilst this influx is generally very helpful, there are cases where it has led to some problems, for example if the standard of English of foreign staff is weak, or if the teaching methods employed do not fit an HEI's culture. Accordingly, as part of the implementation of the HR strategy governors may want to know that management is ensuring that the HR, staff development and quality functions are working together to address any issues in this area.

7.10   There are many advantages of having a broader mix of nationalities among staff:
- It has the potential to rejuvenate the research and teaching capacity of an institution with new ideas from other cultures.
- Having international staff greatly eases the adoption of the 'internationalisation at home' objective. Students are more likely to feel part of a truly international community, and may be able to get relevant advice on study in overseas countries from the staff nationals concerned.
- Having international staff will almost inevitably lead to a less anglo-centric curriculum or style.
- International students may be able to turn to academic staff from their own country in the event of difficulties.
- Research or teaching collaboration may spring from the international staff connections (if these have not been the reason for staff to come here in the first place).

Internationalising the curriculum

7.11   One of the most challenging elements in internationalisation at home is embedding internationalisation into all curricula, and there are several ways in which this can be interpreted[42]:

---

[42] Taken from Caruana, V and Hanstock, J (2003). Internationalising the curriculum; from policy to practice., University of Salford, but they draw on Bremer, L and van der Wende, M eds Internationalising the curriculum in higher education; experiences in the Netherlands. OICHE. The Hague.

- Curricula where the content has been specifically designed for international students.
- Curricula that deal with an international subject.
- Curricula involving an internationally comparative approach.
- Interdisciplinary programmes exploring areas or regions rather than single countries.
- Curricula that prepare students for defined professional careers and where international professional bodies have been involved.
- Foreign language programmes that explicitly address cross-cultural communication and provide skills training.
- Joint or double degree programmes where parts are delivered abroad with local faculty.

An approach favoured by some HEIs is to define the skills and competencies that students have to acquire, once they have studied a curriculum that has been internationalised.

7.12 This area is very much the remit of the senate/academic board, and the details of how the curriculum is internationalised should not concern governors. It is also a topic that tends to be discipline specific. Some professional subjects such as engineering and accountancy have a common international understanding about curricula, while in others (eg humanities and social sciences) many traditional curricula could be euro-centric or even anglo-centric.

7.13 Internationalising the curriculum is a substantial task and will require the active support of faculties or schools. The role of the centre may be limited to developing guidelines on how this is to be done and then monitoring that the change has happened. Thus, as a governor your job is to ask about overall progress in achieving an internationalised curriculum as part of the international strategy, but you should leave the educational aspects to others.

Student and staff mobility

7.14 There is little doubt that a period of study abroad for students is potentially one of the most effective ways of understanding differences in cultures. Therefore, almost all HEIs active in internationalisation list increasing the outwards mobility of their students as a key element in their approach.

7.15 The problem is that the UK's record of getting our students to travel to study is very poor, even though many will have travelled in their vacations or before coming to an HEI. In European programmes such as Erasmus, the students coming to the UK from other EU countries heavily outnumber those from the UK going outwards. In 2008-09 only 10,843 (or 0.43% of all our students) went from the UK on international study or work placements, compared with Germany, Spain and France which each sent over 25,000 students to other countries. UK students also tend to go to English-speaking countries or to English language courses as their language skills are typically poor. It is rare for the percentage of students who travel to exceed 10% of the total student population, although there are some examples of HEIs with a larger proportion. (For example one London HEI has over 25% of its students studying abroad, but this is partly due to the high proportion of language students.) Staff mobility statistics also

"The University of Hong Kong has rebuilt its curriculum from the ground up to embrace 'experiential learning' and internationalisation so as to produce 'global citizens.'"

THE TIMES HIGHER EDUCATION,
4 FEBRUARY 2010

show that UK staff do not travel as much as some of their European counterparts in France, Germany, Poland and Spain.

7.16 Outwards mobility can happen through many routes other than funded programmes such as Erasmus, and the most common is one-to-one collaborations that HEIs themselves arrange. No comprehensive national statistics are available on the numbers who travel in this way, although some partial surveys do collect data[43].

7.17 In practice, in addition to language there are lots of obstacles that explain why UK HEIs are generally not good at getting their students to study abroad:

- The personal circumstances of students, for example an increasing number study part-time and have jobs.
- The additional costs involved, including travel and living.
- Academic staff being unable or unwilling to agree arrangements with overseas HEIs so that the study abroad is compatible with the HEI's own curriculum. Setting up exchange and study agreements and monitoring them can be very time consuming.
- The three year degree courses make it hard to fit in a period of overseas study; with four year programmes it is much easier.
- Some landlords will not refund the rent for the period of study abroad, and in some cases the HEI's own accommodation regulations for its hostels present barriers to mobility.

7.18 However, it has been the policy of all the funding bodies and relevant government departments to achieve more outward mobility, and in some cases funding has been made available to support travel to specific destinations. Several HEIs have set aside their own funds to pay the expenses of students who cannot afford to travel. If your HEI has a policy of encouraging more outwards mobility, as a governor you may want to ask how this will be achieved.

International volunteering

7.19 Another way to encourage students to travel is through international volunteering, in which students use some of their vacation time to work on charitable activities overseas - often in emerging economies. In some HEIs the international office provides administrative support for such activities, although they are nearly always initiated and sponsored by the students union. This is something that a governing body will want to encourage.

7.20 Some HEIs have built up links with particular countries and send regular student groups to work on humanitarian or development aid projects. For example, students in one HEI were so moved by the tsunami disaster in December 2004 that they sent help and then visited the University of Ruhana in Sri Lanka. This has now become a permanent academic link involving staff and research. Of course, HEIs must be clear about liability when students are overseas, and this will be part of standard risk assessment.

---

[43] An academic at Kingston University (Joan-Anton Carbonell) regularly collects statistics from HEIs. The latest survey in 2010 with data from 82 HEIs showed that outwards mobility was increasing slowly, but that the Erasmus route was still the predominant choice because of the funding that it provides.

Self-challenge questions

- Does your HEI want to ensure that its students become global citizens? If so, how does it go about it?
- How effective is your HEI in developing a genuine international community on campus?
- Has there ever been a discussion at the governing body about internationalisation at home, and if not is it wise wholly to depend on the senate or academic board without scrutiny?
- What are the obstacles to greater student mobility overseas and is your HEI taking any steps to ameliorate them?

8. THE ROLE OF THE GOVERNING BODY AND WHAT CAN GO WRONG

8.1 This final chapter pulls together some of the issues raised in detail previously, and provides a brief commentary on the key roles and responsibilities of governors in relation to internationalisation. It also provides some examples of what can - and does - go wrong.

The strategic role of governors

8.2 A theme of this Guide is that although internationalisation has in the past generally not been identified as a key area for governors to watch, it is becoming much more important. This is not just for financial reasons, but also because of the rapid growth in the globalisation of HE, and the surge in numbers of international students crossing borders to study.

8.3 In Chapter 3 internationalisation strategies were explored, and as for all strategic areas the governing body has a responsibility for approval and monitoring, on the advice of the head of institution and other senior managers. Perhaps the main issues concerning an internationalisation strategy from a governing body perspective are:
- How realistic is the strategy, and is it based on sound data?
- Are the risks involved reasonable - including those to reputation - and are they consistent with defined risk appetite?
- Is the strategy financially sustainable, and is it based on full economic cost assumptions?
- Starting and running overseas activities is notoriously time-intensive - is it realistic for the management to deliver the strategy given other pressures?
- Given that its implementation will involve action by deans and heads of department, what is the evidence that they are committed to the strategy?
- Are the proposed performance measures and KPIs appropriate and robust enough?
- Is the HEI making realistic commitments to ensuring and monitoring quality?

8.4 It is very easy for a governing body to make assumptions that an international strategy is appropriate and achievable, given the rise in international student numbers. But as this Guide has shown, internationalisation is complex and may be increasingly challenging. Therefore, if an internationalisation strategy is proposing a rapid expansion in numbers and the speedy development of international partnerships, governors would be justified in querying the extent to which it is realistic and based on robust evidence.

8.5 As noted in Chapter 3, the other aspect of the strategic role of the governing body is, of course, monitoring and measuring the achievement of performance, and as a governor you will want to know how well the HEI is doing with its international strategy. This includes the assessment of quality even if undertaken through the senate or academic board. In addition to the performance indicators suggested in Chapter 3, there is a useful general guide for boards to using KPIs produced by the CUC[44].

44 CUC, 2006, Monitoring Institutional Performance and the Use of Key Performance Indicators, at www.bcu.ac.uk/cuc

Ensuring the appropriate recruitment and support of international students

8.6 Given the importance of income from international students, and also the extensive criticisms about the overly commercial way that some HEIs have recruited, ensuring appropriate and ethical recruiting is a governing body responsibility and not something that should be left to others (although of course a senate/academic board will have a strong interest).

8.7 Based on the issues set out in Chapter 4, some of the areas where governors could usefully ask constructively challenging questions concerning recruitment are:
- The reasons for selecting target countries for recruitment.
- The choice of, and balance between, marketing methods, for example agents, recruitment fairs, advertising, website, private companies for foundation courses.
- The evidence that the HEI is an ethical recruiter.
- The full economic costs of international students, including - but not limited to - marketing and recruitment.
- Steps taken to ensure that UKBA requirements are met.
- How international students are supported, including help given to students on arrival in the UK and for their first few weeks.
- The steps taken to assess international student satisfaction.
- The effectiveness of any alumni network overseas, and how students are encouraged to become ambassadors for the HEI on their return home.

Overseas partnerships

8.8 In Chapter 5 the benefits and risks associated with overseas partnerships were explored, and notwithstanding the real potential benefits there are numerous challenges. Particularly so far as major partnerships are concerned, a governing body has an important responsibility to assure itself - on behalf of the institution - that all is well, and that any risks can be mitigated. Of course, governors will not be in any position to pass judgement on academic issues associated with proposed partnerships, but a board can ask challenging questions about the depth and quality of the partnership selection process, and ensure that suitably rigorous due diligence has been carried out on potential partners.

8.9 Although the details and management of partnerships will not be a matter for the governing body, the areas where governors have a valid interest include:
- Approving the strategy and criteria for selecting overseas partners (including the risk appetite for partnerships).
- How partnerships are reviewed and monitored to ensure effective outcomes in both academic and financial terms.
- The financial sustainability of partnerships and ensuring that there is no cross-subsidy from funding council income.
- Requiring agreed exit strategies to withdraw from less useful collaborations.
- Ensuring that the academic quality of partnerships is monitored through defined quality assurance mechanisms, which include receiving reports on any reviews by the Quality Assurance Agency on relevant offshore and collaborative activities.

"The Secretary of the Council, in consultation with me as Chair, made sure that this project and other overseas commitments were regularly on the Council agenda and that there was therefore a regular opportunity for report and discussion."

CHAIR OF A UNIVERSITY COUNCIL

Setting up and running an offshore activity

8.10   As an area with very substantial risks, this type of internal activity is likely to be of particular concern to governors, and - as noted in Chapter 6 - although the numbers of such campuses are still relatively low, they are likely to increase as more students want to obtain a UK degree without the costs of coming to the UK.

8.11   Although establishing an offshore presence with a partner able to fund the major construction and set-up costs lessens financial risk, it introduces its own set of questions relating to the credibility and financial soundness of the partner, and its reputation. Since any offshore campus will be a long term commitment from the UK institution, there has to be assurance that the partner has a sound long term future and a contractually binding role with the project.

8.12   Governors should be involved with any such proposal from an early stage to ensure strategic fit and due diligence. It will generally be unsatisfactory if a governing body's only involvement is to give formal approval right at the very end of the agreement process, not least because a board turning down a proposed major overseas development after the HEI and partners have shaken hands on the 'deal' might just give rise to a diplomatic incident or two!

8.13   Among the issues that governors may wish to review are:
   - The fit with the internationalisation strategy.
   - The initial feasibility of the venture or proof of concept.
   - The criteria for undertaking due diligence on the partners, and a review of the results.
   - A full risk analysis including reputational risks.
   - Any requirement to create a legal entity in the country concerned and the consequences, for example: a need for share capital; taxation liabilities; the ability to repatriate surpluses; etc.
   - The business plan or financial feasibility study. (Even when relying on partner financing, such a venture will inevitably place a financial requirement on the UK HEI in at least two areas: professional and set-up costs, and the working capital required while the new campus operates at below full capacity. Realistic estimates of these should feature in the business plan.)
   - The HEI's strategy for staffing the offshore activity, for example with UK staff on a temporary basis, with internationally recruited staff, and/or with nationals from the country concerned.
   - An exit strategy in the event of market failure or the emergence of a hostile political environment.
   - The approach to regular and proactive monitoring and evaluation of the venture.

8.14   Of course, once the project is operational the governing body or its committees might expect regular progress reports from the project board or subsidiary company running the venture.

Internationalisation at home

8.15   Although (as noted in Chapter 7) the responsibility for much of this lies elsewhere, there are some areas of legitimate governing body concern, including:

- How activities falling under this heading fit the institutional mission and international strategy.
- Whether the bodies responsible for academic governance (senate, academic board etc) have established policies and expectations for the academic aspects of internationalisation at home, and how progress is assessed.
- What steps management is taking to promote student mobility and what the obstacles are.
- How the HEI will know if it is succeeding in producing graduates who are internationalised.

Reviewing the effectiveness of the management of internationalisation

8.16   As in all other areas, a governing body (or any sub-committee) will need to review the effectiveness of the way that the senior management of internationalisation is undertaken, while - of course - maintaining the separation between governance and management. In particular, governors will wish to know that there are mechanisms for developing, amending and monitoring the internationalisation strategy. In practice, this may include regularly seeking information on issues such as:

- Receiving and discussing annual reports on the performance of internationalisation against agreed KPIs.
- Receiving assurance that effective mechanisms are in place for monitoring and mitigating relevant risks.
- Monitoring the ongoing financial sustainability of internationalisation, both overall and in relation to any significant overseas ventures.
- Ensuring that the management and assurance of quality is being effectively monitored by the various bodies involved in academic governance, and that the outcomes are consistent with institutional intentions.

What can go wrong?

8.17   So finally, what can go wrong? Well, the answer is plenty; and to take a few major examples:

- There have been some well known cases of HEIs in the USA and Australia closing down high profile offshore ventures that were losing money and failing to recruit to target. In some cases they did not act before losses had accumulated.
- Some English HEIs have withdrawn from over-ambitious extensive international franchise operations.
- The Quality Assurance Agency has been critical about aspects of the quality of overseas provision and the way some UK HEIs were assuring quality (see Chapter 5).
- There has been diplomatic embarrassment about some high profile ventures not materialising because of action by one or more partners.
- The international student market can be fickle, for example critical news stories about the treatment of Indian students in Australia in 2008 led to a fall in recruitment in 2009.
- There is the influence of economic trends, for example New Zealand suffered a dramatic fall in the number of Chinese students after an economic crisis.

- Unexpected political developments can turn a potential opportunity into a reputational liability – witness Libya!
- And, of course, just round the corner is the spectre of the consequences of terrorism: one major terrorist attack by an international student in the UK might have huge consequences both in the UK and beyond.

8.18 Therefore, although internationalisation may seem benign to many governors, in practice it is not and is unlikely to be so in the future. So what are the principal risks that governors have to ensure their HEIs address?

- Too great a reliance on a continually increasing income from international students.
- A lack of attention to the quality of the experience of international students and the value for money provided.
- Failure to monitor or vet international students leading to loss of Tier 4 sponsorship.
- Poor control over ventures leading to collaboration with partners with a poor reputation in their country.
- Ignoring the need for full economic cost financial sustainability.
- Risk of currency fluctuation destroying a project's viability.
- Major offshore activities that do not achieve their objectives and damage an HEI's reputation.
- Dramatic political or other major events overseas which could damage the long term viability of any investment. In particular, injury or death of staff or students (as well as being tragic) may have major public relations consequences.
- Developing an uncoordinated set of internationalisation activities that is weakly managed and monitored, so that management does not know what is going on.

A GOVERNOR'S DILEMMA 4:

As a governor, you are very worried about the implications for academic quality (and therefore institutional reputation) of a rapid expansion of international students in the last few years. However, few other governors appear to share your concern, and the PVC responsible seems completely relaxed about the growth and indeed is planning for a further increase in numbers next year. You have looked at the relevant senate/academic board papers and little seems to be raised in them about your concerns, indeed from them you might be justified in thinking that all is well.

However, during informal discussions with academics at social functions over the last year or so, the issue of international students keeps reoccurring, with concerns about poor English language skills, worries about plagiarism and so on. A few have even said (jokingly you hope) that some exam boards are being generous with marks because of the financial benefits of such students being on campus.

You are not sure what to do, and don't want to make a fuss without good reason. What might your next steps be?

ANNEX A: SOME KEY INFORMATION SOURCES

The main information sources likely to be of interest to governors or other readers come from commissioned reports or papers, many of which have been cited in the footnotes to this Guide.

The UK Higher Education International Unit was set up to provide advice to UK HEIs on all aspects of their international activities, and is the largest source of intelligence and research on the topic. Its main product is a fortnightly newsletter freely available on its website at *www.international.ac.uk*. The Unit has also produced several research reports that are helpful, including: *The practice of internationalisation: Managing international activities in universities (2008); The UK's competitive advantage: The market for international research students (2008); UK Universities and Europe: Competition and internationalisation (2009)*. In Spring 2011 the Unit is publishing a report on staffing trans-national education activities with the title '*A UK Guide to staffing strategies in TNE and international operations*'.

A useful overall guide to internationalisation is '*Global Horizons for UK Universities*' published by the Council for Industry and Higher Education in 2007 (*www.international.ac.uk/resources/GLOBAL%20horizons.pdf*). It gives examples of how the various elements of internationalisation are being interpreted in HEIs.

There is more material on international partnerships. The Million+ Group produced a survey of the international partnerships of its members: '*Universities and international partnerships: making a difference*' (2009) (*www.millionplus.ac.uk/research/index*) which explores the barriers to effective partnerships and suggests action. The legal aspects of partnerships have been explored by the UK Higher Education International Unit in '*International partnerships – a legal guide for UK universities*' (2009) (*www.international.ac.uk/login/login.cfm?s_lastCalled=/secure/index.cfm?*), written by Eversheds.

The British Council provides numerous services to support recruitment and partnership, and its web site contains much information which may be relevant to detailed queries, for example market analysis of specific countries. See *www.britishcouncil.org/new/learning*

The UKCISA web site (*www.ukcisa.org.uk*) is also full of useful material on supporting international students.

The Quality Assurance Agency (*www.qaa.ac.uk*) produces reports on institutional audits overseas and reviews of collaborative provision.

Finally, two useful international sources are The American Council on Education and the Institute of International Education. The ACE published guides on aspects of internationalisation between 2007 and 2009, see *www.acenet.edu/Content/NavigationMenu/ProgramsServices/cii/index.htm* under the Center for International Initiatives. The IIE published a Guide in 2010 similar to this one called "International Education as an institutional priority; what every college and university trustee should know", see *www.iie.org/en/Research-and-Publications/Publications-and-Reports/IIE-Bookstore/International-Education-as-an-Institutional-Priority*

ANNEX B: SUGGESTED ANSWERS TO GOVERNORS' DILEMMAS

Dilemma 1 (page 18)

The fact that you think you are being asked to 'rubber stamp' something that has already been determined elsewhere is a common feeling. Before acting, you might reflect on why you think this is so, and there are a number of common reasons. Obviously, one might be management trying to minimise the involvement of governors, but others may be more legitimate even if misguided, for example, trying to maximise the use of time when facing a busy agenda, or trying to minimise the effort required from governors in reading a large pile of papers.

Assuming you decide to raise your concerns, you need to be clear how to do this. You could, of course, just ask for clarification at the governing body meeting, which might be the easiest way of dealing with it; however, there are other - and perhaps better - ways. First, you might contact the clerk/secretary and the chair of the board before the meeting and tell them that you have some concerns (both about the proposed strategy and the way it is to be considered by the governing body), and seek any clarification they can provide. If nothing else, this might allow them to reassign the amount of time required for discussion at the meeting.

If you need further information, you might then want to telephone the appropriate member of the senior management team responsible for the strategy. This will allow you to understand the reasons for the approach taken and may explain the relative timidity of any projections of international students. Governing bodies in HEIs vary in their approach to such contacts between governors and senior managers. In some it is welcomed because of the benefits to open communication it brings (including answering questions of fact at their source), but in others such contact is rare - although if this is the case in your HEI you might want to ask why. If this additional information still doesn't resolve your concerns, then you will need to raise the issue at a governing body meeting, but you will be better informed to do so. Of course, the senior manager concerned may well feel on the defensive if the previous answer has failed to satisfy you!

If the academic community seems reluctant to embark on international initiatives, there may be little that you as a governor can - or should - do in the short term to change this. The issue is one of leadership, and experience from some HEIs has shown that an inspirational head of institution can encourage that institution to think and act more internationally.

Dilemma 2 (page 27)

What you see is very common on UK campuses and is not necessarily a problem, since once international students are in their departments it is very likely that they are mixed in with UK/EU students for their academic work. Thus you are only seeing a very small part of the picture, although if all social activity took place in separate national groups this might cause concern.

Nonetheless you have a point and you should ask the clerk/secretary to let you know of the policies in this area. For example: are departments encouraged to mix nationalities in academic activities such as project groups? what social and cultural programmes does the students union or the institution run to help to integrate different cultural groups? and so on. This is the type of issue that student members of governing bodies can provide useful information about, so you may also want to discuss it informally with them.

If your concerns persist, you could request that some data on the issue is presented as part of any regular monitoring of the internationalisation strategy - if this is not already done. For example, your concerns may be reflected in any surveys of international student satisfaction run by the institution, and your colleagues on the board will all be keen to ensure that international students are satisfied about the quality of their experience. If there is a real problem about integration to be tackled on campus, then some sound data will probably be required for agreed action to be taken.

Dilemma 3 (page 38)

It is a pity that information on this agreement had not been put before the governors earlier in the process, as 'last minute' information on major initiatives often leads to situations like this (whether concerning internationalisation or not). In practice, there are two separate - but related - issues here, one concerning you as an individual and the second you as a governor.

Acting as an individual with knowledge of the country concerned, you should certainly make your thoughts immediately known to the clerk/secretary and the chair and then to the member of the management team who is negotiating this agreement. (See the answer to Dilemma 1 for issues in doing this.) Assuming there are no conflict of interest issues, your contribution here might be limited to just providing information which management might not have, and then leaving them to deal with it as they wish. Of course, subject to the agreement of those involved (and the knowledge of the clerk/secretary) you might continue to have an informal advisory role to management as negotiations proceed. Obviously, this risks breaking the convention about governor involvement in management, but the important issue here is one of transparency and ensuring that managers are ultimately accountable for delivery, with your contribution being only advisory.

In your second role as a governor, you will still need to exercise oversight of the proposal as a whole, and at the outset you should mention to the chair and the clerk/secretary your concern that the board is not getting early enough information about major international ventures. If you do undertake an advisory role to management, this needs to be recognised by the board, and although it will not be a conventional conflict of interest, there will need to be agreement about your contribution on this topic at subsequent board meetings.

Dilemma 4 (page 48)

This is a difficult dilemma and raises an important issue about your role as a governor. The formal position is set out in the financial memorandum with the relevant HE funding body, and the wording varies slightly in the four UK jurisdictions. In England, Hefce requires that "there should be effective arrangements for providing assurance to the governing body that the institution has an effective framework - overseen by its senate, academic board or equivalent - to manage the quality of learning and teaching and to maintain academic standards". Issues in interpreting this are discussed in the separate guide in this series on academic and student matters, and are not repeated here. It follows that - as a governor - it is not your role to be directly involved in determining the potential quality issues raised in the dilemma, but it is your responsibility to ensure that effective processes of academic governance are in place to do that, and to provide the governing body with the assurance required.

In deciding what action - if any - to take, the starting point must be to consider the information you have to hand which consists of little more than personal concerns, and some social gossip. At this point you may decide not to raise the issue, particularly as others seem unconcerned!

Assuming that you do want to take it further, on the information that you have to hand this is not something that most governors would want to raise directly at a board meeting, and you might be better off seeking more information behind the scenes, not least to clarify your own thoughts on what the underlying issues might be. The challenge will be to focus on the strategic and assurance issues and to avoid the academic and operational. The starting point is almost certainly to ask the clerk/secretariat to clarify what discussions have taken place elsewhere about the issues that concern you, and you will probably find that there have been plenty of them - for example, there are regular discussions about how to deal with quality issues in most HEIs. Therefore the issue may simply be one of effective reporting of assurance to the governing body whilst trying to avoid information overload. Given the sensitivities concerned, it may be that the governing body has previously not been clear about the assurance information on academic matters that it requires from others to fulfil its role fully.

This is probably an issue that is best dealt with in the context of a governing body's ongoing review of risks coupled with the achievement of agreed KPIs. Under normal circumstances, the dangers of failing to ensure quality would feature highly on the risk register of most HEIs which were rapidly increasing international student recruitment, and (as with other areas of risk) monitoring this enables governors to undertake their assurance role without direct involvement in operational matters. Therefore if there are issues that concern you after discussion with the clerk, you might propose that this should be considered at the next (perhaps annual) review of the internationalisation strategy and associated risk management arrangements. You could, of course, also raise it informally with the chair of the board and see if she or he agrees with this action.

ANNEX C: AN EXAMPLE INTERNATIONALISATION STRATEGY

*The following is taken (with permission) from the website of the **University of Surrey** and is included as an edited example of an international strategy that is concise, comprehensive and challenging.*

PART A

In recognition of the borderless character of university education, its wide-ranging contribution to economy, culture and society, and in pursuit of the strategic imperative of becoming a top 100 University worldwide by 2017, the University of Surrey presents the following values and principles as part of its multi-dimensional international strategy:

Purpose
The University will be a leading international University in all its activities.

- The University is committed to becoming an international University and to be in the top 100 Universities in the world by 2017. To that end, it incorporates the following aims in its International Strategy:
- To internationalise the educational, cultural and social experience of all students, faculty and staff irrespective of location such that the University's contributions to learning, teaching, research and enterprise gain real and concrete expression in professional and academic experience, relevance and international impact.
- To give the University substantive international reach through strategic partnerships with quality institutions and public and private research funding bodies and other relevant organisations.
- To promote international influence, reputation and visibility through a network of influencers in international, national and transnational government and non-governmental organisations.

1. Global Networks: the Institutional Dimension
The University will continue to develop its network of formal institutional partnerships in the form of 'Global Partnership Networks', Strategic Partnerships and Bilateral Accords.

2. Global Graduates: the Learning Dimension
The University will introduce a step-change in the international experience of all its students irrespective of the place of delivery. To this end it will promote mobility, raise intercultural awareness and make the curriculum (contents, mode of delivery and assessment) responsive to the needs of global society, culture and economy.

3. Global faculty and staff: the Research, Enterprise and Teaching Dimension
The University will continue to foster the international experience of all faculty and staff whether based in the United Kingdom or elsewhere. To this end it will promote mobility and raise intercultural awareness and make pedagogy responsive to the needs of the global society, culture and economy while promoting research and enterprise collaboration with its strategic partners.

PART B

I) Context

The University must keep pace with significant changes in the global higher education context:

1.	UK factors including the changes in University funding mechanisms, student demographics, Government education policy, student and employer demands.

2.	International European factors including the consequences of the Bologna Process and the Lisbon Accord.

3.	International factors including increasingly competitive markets, increasing quality and quantity of international providers outside the UK and rapidly changing patterns of demand and demographic change (e.g. India and China).

II) Purpose

•	The University is committed to being a leading international University in all its activities.

•	The University is committed to becoming an international University in word and deed and to be in the top 100 Universities in the world by 2017 at the latest. To that end it incorporates the following aims in its international strategy:

•	To internationalise the educational, cultural and social experience of all students, including home students, faculty and staff such that the University's contributions to learning, teaching, research and enterprise gain real and concrete expression in professional and academic experience, relevance and international impact.

•	To give the University substantive international reach through strategic partnerships with quality institutions and public and private research funding bodies.

•	To promote international influence, reputation and visibility through a network of influencers in international, national and transnational government and non-governmental organisations.

1. Global Networks: the Institutional Dimension
Global Partnership Networks (GPN)
Strategic Partnerships and Bilateral Accords
The University will develop its network of formal institutional partnerships, developing the International Partnership Implementation Plan agreed by EB in July 2006. The criteria for selection of a partner will include:

a.	Broad academic match, so that more than two Faculties of the University are matched by critical mass of activity in the partner.

b.	A high quality international profile and reputation on its own account.

c.	Location in an area of research-driven economic growth.

d.	Good relations with local industry and government.

e.	Orientation towards professional programmes and research-led teaching.

f.	A culture of student and staff mobility.

g.	Sustainability.

h.	Potential for strategic network building.

Areas of interest have been prioritised according to the need for geostrategic reach. For the period 2007-09 the following countries are priorities: USA, India, Brazil, the countries of southern Africa, Malaysia and China (including Hong Kong SAR).

Milestones:

1. Extension of Global Partnership Network membership to three members by 2008 and four by 2009.
2. Extension of strategic partnerships to two by end of 2009 (target partners: India, China).
3. Central database of contacts created by mid-2008, reports of meetings available and annual plan of activity agreed.

2. Global Graduates: the Learning and Living Dimension

International Mobility

Student mobility programmes covering EU and International Exchange and Study Abroad will be further developed and/or established in appropriate Faculties.

Collaborative Programmes

The University will actively promote and support dual and joint awards with partner institutions for undergraduate, postgraduate taught and doctoral students.

Curriculum Design

The University will make its curriculum relevant to the demands of the international graduate economy. Internationalisation of the curriculum will comprise a range of measures including the Global Graduate Award in either International or European Politics or a Modern Language for first or second-year undergraduate students.

The Global Graduate Award

The Supplement will be awarded on successful completion of one 10-credit undergraduate module at level 1 and/or level 2 from International or European Politics or a range of over ten European languages (including French, German, Spanish or Russian) and non-European languages (including Arabic, Japanese and Mandarin) to reflect the rapidly growing importance of both European integration and globalisation for all Surrey's graduates. This includes English as a Modern Foreign Language for our non-native English speaking students. The Global Graduate Award will also automatically be recorded on the candidate's degree-level (EU and UNESCO-initiated) 'European Diploma Supplement', when this is introduced at Surrey post-SITS introduction from 2008. Students and staff will also be encouraged to benefit from the cultural and linguistic diversity of Surrey by forming language and culture learning partnerships as part of the University's Tandem Learning Network.

Approaches to Learning and Teaching

In recognition of the cultural specificity of learning and teaching traditions internationally, this strategy highlights the need for a rethinking of pedagogy and support for all students including, for example, the introduction of case study models in all disciplines by 2010; establishment of intra-faculty websites to showcase good practice and innovation; establishment of a timetable for change, potentially initiating incentives for staff development.

Targets

- Introduction of credit-bearing Global Graduate Award in Mandarin Chinese, Spanish and International or European Politics from 2010.
- Introduction of credit-bearing Global Graduate Award module in other languages from 2011.

Milestones:
1.   Pilot scheme Global Graduate Award introduction (Mandarin) from 2009.

Professional Training

The University will ensure that the benefits of the professional training year for undergraduates, and opportunities for industrial placement for postgraduate taught students, are available equally to UK and international students, and that placements are available outside the United Kingdom. Placements for non-UK students should be available inter alia in the students' countries of origin. In addition, careers advice is to be extended to all Surrey students.

Target:
•   Establishment of professional training opportunities through GPN members and Strategic Partners from 2009.

Milestones:
1.   Number and range of placements, uptake of placements.

Environment and Experience

The University will seek to ensure that the student community is an open and integrated society from which none are excluded by cultural challenges. To that end, facilities will be provided for social, recreational, and cultural activity, in ways which permit free and inclusive association between students of different backgrounds and in pursuit of international understanding.

Milestones:
1.   Intercultural awareness workshops organised with Student Services, Corporate Services and the MFC throughout the year.
2.   Design and implementation of accommodation policy to facilitate multicultural community-building.
3.   Carbon management policies to offset carbon footprint of international activities.

3. Global Faculty and Staff

Research Activity

The University will promote and support the exploration of opportunities for high-quality joint research and collaborative bidding to international funding agencies with GPN members, Strategic Partners and other overseas and other European academic collaborators.

International Academic Participation

The University will encourage and support participation at quality international conferences and policy fora, using incentives to encourage participation in events which will enhance reputation or influence.

Consultancy and Advice/Exploitation of intellectual property overseas

In making and implementing policies and procedures for promotion and reward, the University will have regard to international consultancy and policy advice by members of staff.

The University will take action, where appropriate, to secure successful exploitation of its intellectual property outside the UK market.

Enhancing Performance in an international environment
This strategy also requires the preparation and development of faculty and staff in how to work effectively at an international University as well as working internationally. The inclusion of international activity will be explored for future staff contracts and consideration given to the inclusion of incentives, recognition and reward for international activities (such as teaching abroad/staff mobility) in the SDR process.

Staff Experience and Staff Exchange
The experience of international staff working at Surrey will be incorporated into the University's international activity and a framework established and resourced to ensure that staff exchange (both inward and outward) is valued and encouraged. Such exchange will encompass GPN members, Strategic Partnerships and other partners. Surrey will provide a supportive environment for international (including non-UK European) colleagues in their development as researchers, teachers and administrators.

Student Recruitment
The Student Recruitment Office will extend its target range for direct recruitment to include the whole Indian sub-continent, the Middle East, West Africa, Eastern Europe and the non-EU Bologna countries. This will be achieved principally by shifting resources to the support of agents (including interview tours) and working with partners such as Study Group and their sub-agents. The range of countries addressed will be kept under review by the Student Recruitment Office/ISO in consultation with the International Relations Office and Planning Committee and informed by intelligence from central marketing.

Dual Masters and doctoral programmes will be developed with GPN or Strategic Partners. The increasingly popular '1+3' MSc + PhD route will be marketed as an integrated programme with pre-set progression requirements rather than two independent programmes. International students will be encouraged to attend English Language courses in LTS in partial satisfaction of normal IELTS requirements.

April 2008
Updated September 2009

ABOUT THE AUTHOR:

John Fielden

Has practised as a management consultant in higher education policy and management since 1969. In 1993 he set up the Commonwealth Higher Education Management Service (CHEMS), the research and consultancy service of the Association of Commonwealth Universities. He now runs CHEMS Consulting as an independent consultancy and has carried out over 270 education projects in over 42 countries. His main specialisms are HE policy studies for agencies and governments, internationalisation and governance issues, and the role of the private sector in higher education. International clients have included the World Bank, UNESCO, British Council and many education ministries and universities throughout the world.

ABOUT THE SERIES EDITOR:

Allan Schofield

Allan Schofield runs The Higher Education Consultancy Group, and is a Key Associate of the Leadership Foundation for Higher Education. He is one of the most experienced consultants in the UK specialising in higher education management and governance, and during the past 20 years has worked in more than 80 universities and colleges. He has worked extensively with almost all the main UK national HE agencies on a wide range of policy and evaluation studies. In the last few years he has been heavily involved in many of the national activities to enhance the governance of higher education in the UK, and has been project director of several LFHE-CUC projects. In 2009 he also led a national review of governance in English further education. Internationally he has undertaken substantial work for the World Bank, British Council, the Asian Development Bank, the Association of Commonwealth Universities, and other international organisations.